SESSIONS WITH PETER

Smyth & Helwys Publishing, Inc.
6316 Peake Road
Macon, Georgia 31210-3960
1-800-747-3016
© 2006 by Smyth & Helwys Publishing
All rights reserved.
Printed in the United States of America.

The paper used in this publication meets the minimum
requirements of American National Standard for Information
Sciences—Permanence of Paper for Printed Library Materials.

Library of Congress Cataloging-in-Publication Data

Shelton, Sarah Jackson.
Sessions with Peter / Sarah Jackson Shelton.
p. cm.
Includes bibliographical references and index.
ISBN 1-57312-454-0 (pbk. : alk. paper)
1. Bible. N.T. Peter--Commentaries.
I. Title.
BS2795.53.S54 2006
227'.9207--dc22

2005037665

Sessions *with*
Peter

Discovering God's *Encouragement* for the *Christian Journey*

Sarah Jackson Shelton

SMYTH&HELWYS
PUBLISHING, INCORPORATED • MACON, GEORGIA

Dedication

This book is lovingly dedicated to the courageous congregation of
Baptist Church of the Covenant and to Lloyd, David, and Dannelly
for their constant love and encouragement.

Special appreciation is expressed to Betty Lou Jackson Land,
Susan Palmer, Jack Brymer, and Sarah Wilson, who served as
my editing committee

Table of Contents

Session One 1
Introducing Peter: Tangible Encouragement

Session Two 7
More Valuable than Gold
1 Peter 1

Session Three 15
The Family Crest
1 Peter 2:1–3:12

Session Four 23
Not Until You Bless Me
Genesis 32:22-31; 1 Peter 3:8-22; 4:1-6

Session Five 31
Practicing Hospitality
1 Peter 4:7-11; Matthew 10:40-42; Hebrews 13:1-2

Session Six...41
Greeting with a Kiss
1 Peter 5

Session Seven 47
The Ladder of Virtues
2 Peter 1:1-15

Session Eight 53
Standing in the Thin Places: A Window to Mystery
2 Peter 1:16-21; Matthew 17:1-8

Session Nine 61
Waterless Springs
2 Peter 2

Session Ten 67
Waiting on the Lord
2 Peter 3:1-18

Introducing Peter: Tangible Encouragement

At one time in my family's history, all of us were scattered. One sister lived in Alabama; one sister lived in South Carolina; our brother lived in Colorado; and I lived in Kentucky, attending seminary. Our mother would write to us faithfully. Her letters were full of family news, menus that she prepared to serve guests or take to shut-ins, and general information about her activities with Dad. These letters came as often as three times a week. They began with "Dear Ones" and ended with "Love and Kisses, Mother." They were single-spaced and took up an entire page. Mother typed them using carbon paper and rotated the original between us. She sometimes included words of wisdom, but mostly her letters reminded us that we were never far from her thoughts and prayers. When we received her letters, we knew we were holding tangible encouragement.

When the believers received Peter's letters, I think they received tangible encouragement as well. First and Second Peter comprise two of the seven general letters found in the New Testament. This means these letters were read in one congregation and then passed to another community of faith within the same geographical region. Because the letters rotated, they are not addressed to one particular church but to the larger Christian community.

The addressees are referred to as "exiles of the Diaspora in Pontus, Galatia, Cappadocia, Asia, and Bithynia" (1 Pet 1:1). In the Old Testament, any exile was considered a continuation of Israel's separation from their true home. It usually meant Jews were forced to live as slaves among Gentiles in foreign lands, where they were tempted to adopt new cultural mores and religious practices. They experienced civil strife and persecution from friends, associates, and family. When local authorities were not harassing the Jews, others who longed for these believers to return to their former habits often taunted them. This alien status is best described in the *Testament of Asher* 7:2: "You will be scattered to the four corners of the earth; in the dispersion you shall be regarded as worthless, like useless water, until such time as the Most High visits the earth."[1]

Through the years, the idea of exile has evolved so that contemporary interpreters view those exiled to mean Christians separated from Christ because we live in this world.[2] We too know the temptation of returning to our lives before we knew Christ and of losing hope for redemption in the face of persecution because of our beliefs. The purpose of 1 and 2 Peter remains true even today. Rather than a social justice or political appeal, Peter's purpose is a theological one. With a vision set forth of the transformation that occurs within us because of our conversion, Peter constantly reminds us to respond to harassment with holiness and rebirth and sanctification. The ultimate hope is that how we respond to our persecutors will bring about salvation in those who taunt us. Just like the example of Jesus, our call is to be found faithful to God's grace in spite of persecution, temptation, alienation, or social oppression.[3] As it was to its original audience, Peter's encouragement for us to stay true to our Christian beliefs is a welcome drink of cold water in a spiritual desert.

The authorship of 1 and 2 Peter is greatly debated. While tradition dictates that Peter wrote the first letter (about AD 64), few scholars would support this as fact for 2 Peter. The dramatic literary differences and the strong dependence on Jude as a source for the second letter cause most to believe 2 Peter was written much later and by one who viewed himself as among the last of the apostolic witnesses. The major issue in the second letter deals with Gnostic false teachings regarding the second coming of Christ, which likely dates the letter to about AD 140–150. Regardless of the authorship issue, 2 Peter was written in an effort to recall the spirit of Peter's teachings and to provide some stability during a time of turmoil caused by false teaching.[4]

When our mother died, one of my jobs was to clean out her desk. As I went through drawers and organized paper clips, you can imagine my delight in finding three years' worth of letters of which she had saved copies. These letters were duplicated and given to all of my siblings. As I handled those pages of onionskin, I came across another letter she had saved. I recognized my own handwriting and, upon seeing the date, remembered that I had written this letter during my seminary days. It was written to thank my parents for all of the educational opportunities and experiences they had afforded me. Mother had saved it all those years for her own tangible encouragement.

As we make this journey through 1 and 2 Peter, may his words reach across the centuries to bring tangible encouragement to us.

Prayer

O Lord our God, we thank you for the divine encouragement we still receive through these ancient texts and through the lives of those in exile around the world today. Amen.

Exercises for Spiritual Reflection

1. Take time to read 1 and 2 Peter. Write down all the phrases that offer encouragement.

_____

_____

_____

_____

_____

_____

_____

_____

2. Think of a time when you were "in exile." How did someone touch your life to give you encouragement?

_____

_____

_____

_____

_____

_____

_____

_____

3. Make a list of the people you know who are "in exile," i.e., who need a word of encouragement.

_____

_____

_____

_____

_____

_____

_____

4. Choose one person from your list above and write a letter of encouragement. Let 1 Thessalonians 4:18 be your guide: "Therefore comfort/encourage one another with these words." Keep a copy of your letter. If there is a response, keep it with your letter. How might this experience challenge you to write letters of encouragement to others on your list?

_____

_____

_____

_____

_____

_____

_____

_____

5. Pray for the people on your list. Keep a record of how your prayers are answered.

_____

_____

_____

_____

_____

_____

_____

_____

NOTES

[1] Pheme Perkins, *First and Second Peter, James, and Jude,* Interpretation: A Bible Commentary for Teaching and Preaching (Louisville: John Knox Press, 1995), 13.

[2] Ibid., 12.

[3] Richard Spencer, "Letters of Peter," *Mercer Dictionary of the Bible,* ed. Watson E. Mills et al. (Macon GA: Mercer University Press, 1990), 678.

[4] Perkins, *First and Second Peter, James, and Jude,* 160.

It was the worst idea our mother ever had. Concerned that we were not eating properly and that we would grow up deficient of essential vitamins, our mother ordered boxes and boxes of supplements. We were to take them at every meal and before we went to bed. There was one problem. Being the youngest of the children, I had not yet learned the fine art of swallowing pills. Mother was not deterred. Instead, she purchased a large brown bottle of iron tonic. I was to take it two times a day. I would stand beside her desk, watching as she pulled out the spoon and carefully poured the tonic. I would swallow the vile liquid, and she would pop a mint into my mouth to take away the horrible taste. (Of course, I no longer take liquid vitamins, but I still do not like the taste of those mints!)

The day came when I had had enough. I purposefully took the bottle and hid it behind a door in a back hallway of our house. When it was time for doling out the awful stuff, my mother could not find the bottle. This went on for days. My brother, a little more honest in his estimation of me, was immediately suspicious. Speculations were abundant, but I was not opening my mouth for confession or for taking vitamins! Eventually, our housekeeper uncovered the hiding place when she mopped the floor.

Mother walked me to the hiding place. My brother followed us. He taunted all the while: "Are you gonna spank her? Are you? Huh? Huh? Huh?" Mother showed me the bottle. I confessed. My brother continued to pester in order to find out the punishment. Finally, Mother turned to my brother and said, "You need to be quiet." Then she placed her hand on my shoulder, looked at me, and responded to my brother, "Don't you know she is as good as gold?"

At that moment, I felt my mother's blessing wash all over me. In the face of sure and certain punishment, her expression of love was undeserved. It was pure gift. It was grace. (And the bottle of tonic vanished!)

The audience to which Peter writes is in a similar situation. Some were having a hard time swallowing the new expectations of the Christian ethic, especially while living far from their homeland. In addition to giving up old habits that characterized their lives before becoming Christians, they were expected to maintain a level of behavior that gave witness to the Christians' faith, so that even in the face of harassment, others would be brought to salvation. They found themselves in a foreign land with little cultural familiarity. They were being employed as slaves and taunted by residents who regarded their abilities as inferior and placed them at the lowest level of social structure. These Christians faced hostility from friends, family members, and associates in the form of harassment and persecution. When they were not being harassed, they were treated as if they were of no value. It was almost as if they were invisible and nameless.

The plight of Peter's audience reminds me of a story Fred Craddock tells about his experience leading a chaplains' retreat while at Fort Belvoir, Virginia.[1]

> They treated me very well. I ate in the officers' mess, and the soldiers who waited on us wore sort of sad green fatigues. However, on their uniforms where normally a soldier would have a nametag, there was nothing. That name badge had been ripped off. I said to the fellow waiting on me, a very nice young man, "I see you don't have on your nametag. What's your name?" He didn't answer me. I said to the officer beside me, "Why didn't he answer? What's his name?"
>
> "He doesn't have one," the officer said.
>
> "What do you mean? Give me a break here. What's his name?"
>
> "He has no name," the officer repeated.
>
> "Who are these people waiting on us?" I asked.
>
> "Conscientious objectors."
>
> This was during the Vietnam War, and these were conscientious objectors. They do not exist, they have no names, so eat your lunch. Can you believe that? No names.

Verse 1 of chapter 1 seems to imply this same perception and attitude. Peter begins by distinguishing himself as an apostle—one who had witnessed the activities of Jesus, thus giving him authority. Those addressed are merely mentioned as those who are in exile, in other words, those who are of an inferior status. In our day and age, they could be people who are seen but are never heard; people whose existence is easier to ignore than to recognize and respect; people whose skin color, accent, lifestyle, personal choices, or background experiences cause us to be uninterested in knowing their names or, if we regard them at all, provoke antagonistic, culturally biased remarks.

This type of introduction, then, makes verse 2 all the more surprising and meaningful. For while the audience is composed of those who are in exile, Peter makes it clear that they are chosen. They are destined. They are an elect people. This makes them more special than Peter! They are special because of God's love and their response to that love through their faith. It is a faith more valuable than gold.

The theme of the letters is found in 1:3. It states that we have been born anew to a living hope. There is much reassurance that Jesus has paid everyone's ransom money in order to bring freedom, even to those currently in slavery. Peter quickly moves his readers from the status of exiled foreigners to members of a household to which they can belong, a family that treasures their presence, and a future that awaits them with hopeful promise. Rather than marginal people, they are now seen for the worth they possess in the eyes of God.

In our downtown church, we often find that transients sleep on the back porch of our facilities. Rarely do our guests stay for more than one night. I noticed, however, that one man stayed several weeks. It was cold, and so I began what would become our friendship with cups of hot coffee. I learned that his name was Andrew. Andrew was a Vietnam War veteran and had no desire to stay in a shelter or for me to contact his family. He was, however, open to a relationship.

After several "back-porch picnics" and some conversation, I invited Andrew to come to church. The first Sunday he came, my children watched in amazement. He was wearing the black sweatpants that had been a part of their Halloween costume just a few months before! Andrew sat quietly through the service. I introduced him as my guest. At the end of the service, one of the men in the congregation took Andrew to Sunday school and then to lunch. This became their routine every Sunday Andrew attended and often included meeting for breakfast at least one day during the week. I wondered if this relationship was the first one Andrew had experienced that did not require something in return. It was purely gift. It was seeing another not as a homeless person or a transient or a beggar. It was seeing another with God's eyes as worthy and lovely. It was watching 1 Peter 1:22 in action: "Love one another with a pure heart."

Over the course of the next year, we connected Andrew with a social worker at the local veteran's hospital. Andrew would come to worship donning white patent leather shoes on his feet and a large silver cross around his neck. He carried the largest Bible I have ever seen! Anytime we met up with one another, he would answer my questions with the same words. Regardless of if he was under the weather or had had his things stolen or if he had been beaten up, Andrew would find a way to respond with, "Oh, Pastor, I am just praising God for this church and for you."

Andrew has since moved away, but every now and then I get a note in the mail. His letters serve as a reminder of his prayers and his appreciation for being treated as a child of God.

These experiences with Andrew have taught me valuable lessons. First, they speak to me of the importance of valuing each person as God's wondrous creation. Secondly, they speak to me of the power of our actions and attitudes, especially in difficult situations, to bring salvation to others.

Peter consistently puts the example of Jesus before us as we continue to read the first chapter. The model is that of the righteous one who suffers. It is pertinent because many who read the letters found themselves in the same situation. Because of their Christian faith, they were being persecuted. With faith comes an element of truthfulness that often stirs up anger and dissension. Our goal is not to be found righteous when this happens, but to be found faithful. The ways we respond to difficulties—hopefully as Christ would respond—is our strongest testimony to the power of the gospel. The danger is that the issues at hand will shake our faith from its foundation rather than be an opportunity to witness to the glory of God.

Peter, therefore, ends the chapter with a call to holiness. He gives direct exhortations to be obedient children who follow the example of our divine Parent. Our ultimate goal is to be holy as God is holy. It is not judgment. It is a directive to which we are constantly striving.

While Peter's audience was truly in exile, few of us have had this experience. However, we often experience a figurative exile because of our faith. We live in a world in which we no longer fit because of our faith. We are stranded here, in exile if you will, until the second coming of Christ. So while we are in this waiting mode, we set the goal of holiness and live for perfection. We live with the assurance found in verses 2 and 21 of chapter 1—in other words, that our peace will come from our faith and hope in God.

The chapter ends with the governing commandment to love one another from the heart. When the world rejects us, how comforting it is to know that there is a place and a group of people who love us constantly, earnestly, and with perseverance.

When my parents traveled to South America, they sent their children to stay with aunts and uncles and grandparents. As my mother prepared my brother and sister to ride the train to Georgia, she settled them into their seats with books, crayons, a sack lunch, and a few other surprises. As she hugged and kissed them good-bye, my preschool-aged brother reached up to hold her face and said, "Don't forget where am I."

When we are in exile, we have a holy God who never forgets where we are. In fact, Peter's assurances remind us that we are chosen, called to live with purpose, and that we, as well as our faith, are indeed as good as gold.

Prayer

O Lord our God, hold our faces in your hands so that we become ever more aware of your constant, encouraging presence. Amen.

Exercises for Spiritual Reflection

1. The letters of 1 and 2 Peter were addressed to individuals living temporarily in Roman provinces. Most were Jews living outside of Israel, or they were Gentile converts. These people felt bereft. They had no privileges. They grieved for home but instead found themselves in foreign lands and treated with little, if any, respect. While you may have never been physically displaced, you may have experienced spiritual displacement. Describe a time when you felt as if you were an "alien," i.e., a person in spiritual exile.

_____
_____
_____
_____
_____
_____
_____

2. Consider Peter's faith journey. Read Matthew 8:14-17; 16:13-20; Mark 1:16-20; 3:13-16; 5:37; 8:31-33; 14:26-33, 66-72; 16:1-8; John 21:1-19. How might these experiences give Peter a background to relate to the needs and concerns of his exiled readers?

_____
_____
_____
_____
_____
_____

3. Describe a person or event that gave you a sense of belonging or blessing. If you cannot recall an incident of this sort, what would have helped you feel included?

_____
_____
_____
_____
_____

4. How might this experience, or lack of one, be used to help you take on Peter's role of encourager?

_____

_____

_____

_____

_____

_____

5. Verse 3 says we are "born anew" because of "God's mercy" and for the purpose of becoming "living hope." List ways you desire to be an example of "living hope."

_____

_____

_____

_____

_____

_____

6. How is your faith more precious than gold?

_____

_____

_____

_____

_____

_____

7. Read verses 13 and following. Make a list of the mandates we are to follow as believers.

_____

_____

_____

_____

_____

_____

8. Peter speaks of an inheritance that is imperishable, undefiled, and unfading. It is guarded for us in heaven. What sort of spiritual inheritance will you leave behind?

_____

_____

_____

_____

_____

_____

9. List the recipients of your spiritual inheritance. Think beyond immediate recipients.

_____

_____

_____

_____

_____

_____

NOTE

[1] Fred B. Craddock, "How Long Does Easter Last?" _The Cherry Log Sermons_ (Louisville: Westminster John Knox Press, 2001), 105.

The Family Crest

1 Peter 2:1–3:12

Peter continues his words of encouragement in chapter 2. Just as the craftsman looks through building materials to choose the defining cornerstone, so God has selected us to be living stones in the spiritual house that Jesus defines with his presence as the cornerstone. The theme of being chosen as part of the royal priesthood, God's own people, develops throughout this chapter. Our distinction is explained in verse 10: "Once you were no people but now you are God's people; once you had not received mercy but now you have received mercy."

The transformation mercy brings requires us to change our behavior. Holiness demands that we set evil aside. We are challenged to take off the things that characterized our past life just like we would take off soiled clothes. Because Peter is concerned that salvation is always put forth through our actions, he does not want us to emulate the behaviors of those who harass us; in other words, he advises not to participate in sins of the spirit like malice, guile, insincerity, envy, and slander (2:1).

As cherished members of God's holy nation and royal priesthood, we are set apart to declare the wonderful deeds of God. Traditionally, this has meant we are to sing God's praises in worship. Peter's main focus, however, is that the believer's life and words will also be a testimony of God's glory. If we are able to live in this way, then others might be drawn into the family of faith through our living witness.[1]

The next sections deal with the specifics of how Christians are to live in a non-Christian world. It is an ethical call to action so that as displaced people, we will know how to live lives of holiness before those who harass and threaten us. These codes of conduct begin with a general admonition in verses 11 and 12. They move to specific activity in the verses that follow.

Because many of the letters' original recipients had been brought into a foreign land as slaves, Peter has a consistent theme that deals with being subjected to another's authority.

- Be subject to every human institution (emperor, governor), 2:13.
- Be submissive to your master, 2:18.
- Wives are to be submissive to their husbands, 3:1.
- Husbands are to live considerately with their wives, 3:7.

Pheme Perkins in his commentary on 1 and 2 Peter says:

> The most difficult elements in this section of the letter for Christians today are the repeated exhortations to be obedient to superiors. Bitter experience has taught Christians that such advice often permits dictatorships to abuse the weak and the rich to oppress the poor, and makes the church complicitous in social justice. . . . I Peter never says that it is right for a master to beat his slaves irrationally—but that rebellious behavior would not gain anything. Therefore, I Peter counsels taking Christ as one's model and submit to the treatment as a way of gaining what dignity and honor one can from a situation that is less than ideal.[2]

The consistency of the letters' theme is evident. Our conduct must show others the validity of our Christian beliefs. Christ and his sufferings are consistently put forward as the model for our response to unjust situations. Just like Christ, we do not threaten or respond to insults with more insults. Instead, we anticipate the judgment of God. While waiting for God to act, we gain hope from our inheritance as children of God, confidence from our salvation, and support from the community of faith to which we belong. We should, therefore, live as servants of God and honor all people.

The first several verses of chapter 3 discuss how to honor those with whom we live. Women are encouraged to develop the inward, imperishable beauty of a gentle and quiet spirit. This is more precious to God than a jewel. Likewise, husbands are to honor the individuality of each person. This mutual submission takes away the sting of a hierarchical model that places the husband over the wife. Both work together within their relationship, their family, and the larger community to share love, compassion, and humility. Retaliation is not acceptable. Rather, believers are encouraged to give blessings or quiet words of respect and sympathy.

These calls to action remind us that our behavior should be so consistent that others will know what to expect in our responses. The dictates of our faith should be as obvious as if we wore our character on our sleeves.

Prayer

O Lord our God, make our actions and attitudes consistent with the model of servanthood you lived through Jesus Christ our Lord and Savior. Amen.

Exercise for Spiritual Reflection

For centuries, family crests or coats of arms have served as distinguishing symbols for families. A tradition that developed during the Holy Wars and found its maturity with Feudalism, heraldry moved from a military status symbol to a mark of noble status. Peter defines us as a royal priesthood and then gives specific behaviors to identify us as members of this holy family; hence it may be worth our time to consider what might compose our spiritual family crest.

An example of a coat of arms is provided below, as well as a small listing of what some symbols represent. Remember that a coat of arms, in reality, gave identification only to the one person who developed it. So family members might accept it as representative of them all, or each member might have different symbols upon their crests.[3]

The shield shape may vary, just as the elements on it are chosen to define the character of the individual who carries it. Color choice continues to give symbolic representation. The shield below is divided into four parts to give further identification. The helmet and crest appear above the shield. The helmet gives rank identification and the century represented. The other elements, such as the supporter and wreath, are decorative in nature.

Coat of Arms Imagery[4]

Colors	
Gold	generosity and elevation of mind
Silver/white	peace and sincerity
Red	warrior or martyr; magnanimity
Blue	truth and loyalty
Green	hope, joy, and loyalty in love
Black	constancy or grief
Purple	royal majesty, sovereignty, justice
Orange	worthy ambition
Maroon	patient in battle, yet victorious

Symbols

Anchor	hope, religious steadfastness
Angels	dignity, glory, bearer of joyful news
Bear	strength, ferocity in protection
Beaver	industry and perseverance
Boar	bravery and hospitality
Buck/deer	peace and harmony
Bull/buffalo	valor, bravery, generosity
Candle/lamp	light, life, spirituality
Chains	reward for service
Church	religion, faith, community
Column	fortitude and constancy
Crook	watchfulness, faith, authority
Cross	faith, Christianity, service
Crown	royal, authority
Dog	courage, vigilance, loyalty
Dolphin	swiftness, diligence, salvation
Dove	loving constancy and peace, bearer of good news, Holy Spirit
Eagle	noble nature, strength, bravery
Flowers	hope and joy
Hammer	honor
Hand	pledge of faith, sincerity
Harp	tempered judgment
Heart	intense, burning affection
Helmet	wisdom, security, protection
Ivy	strong and lasting friendship
Keys	guardianship, dominion
Lamb	gentleness, patience under suffering
Lightning bolt	swiftness, power
Lion	dauntless courage
Mermaid	eloquence
Palm	victory, justice, royal honor
Scroll	scholarly
Snake	wisdom
Star	celestial goodness, noble person
Sun	glory, splendor, fountain of life
Wheel	fortune, cycle of life
Wings	swiftness, protection

Our actions should be as obvious as if we had them presented on a shield, visible to all we encounter. Follow the steps below to develop your spiritual coat of arms.

1. Fill in your name beneath the shield.

2. Read through chapters 1 and 2. Choose a phrase or paraphrase a verse to be your motto. Record your motto under your name.

3. Use color to create a wreath.

4. As a "soldier of Christ's in truth arrayed," design your helmet.

5. Look through the list of symbols and choose supporters and a crest.

6. Read 2:13-17. In square 1, what might you include to symbolize your servanthood? How will you live as a servant of God and others so that all will be honored?

_____

_____

_____

_____

_____

_____

7. Read 2:18-25. In square 2, what might you include to symbolize your responses to persecution? How will you respond to your criticizers?

_____

_____

_____

_____

_____

_____

8. Read 3:1-7. In square 3, what might you include to symbolize your family relationships? How might you show a gentle and quiet spirit with your family? How could you treat other family members so that

they would know they are precious in God's sight? (Family members can be considered to be biological family or church family.)

_____

_____

_____

_____

_____

_____

9. Read 3:8-12. In square 4, what might you include to symbolize giving a blessing to others rather than retaliation? How will we give a blessing to others at home, at church, at work, and within the community?

_____

_____

_____

_____

_____

Share the meaning of your crest with a study group member, family member, or friend.

NOTES

[1] Pheme Perkins, *First and Second Peter, James, and Jude,* Interpretation: A Bible Commentary for Teaching and Preaching (Louisville: John Knox Press, 1995), 41.

[2] Ibid., 46.

[3] "A Brief History of Heraldry," http://www.fleurdelis.com/coatofarms.htm.

[4] "The Meanings Behind the Symbols: Family Crests, Blazons, Coat of Arms, Personalized," http://www.fleurdelis.com/meanings.htm.

My Coat of Arms

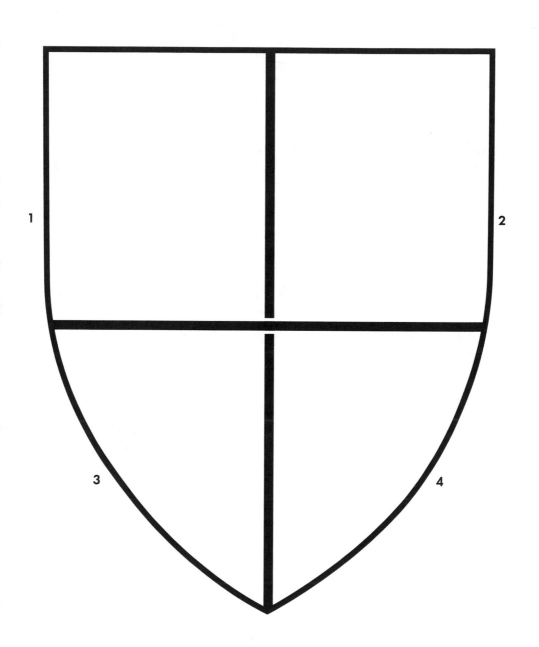

Not Until You Bless Me

Genesis 32:22-31, 1 Peter 3:8-22; 4:1-6

Because of my love for family stories, I have always been fascinated with the stories of Genesis. The majority of this book tells the story of one family system. It covers four generations: Abraham and Sarah, Isaac and Rebekah, Jacob and Rachel, and finally Joseph and his brothers. While each character contains a host of preaching material, one of the most dynamic and complex individuals is Jacob, the youngest twin son of Isaac and Rebekah.

Just as the participants of this family history get settled into tradition and are lulled into lack of expectation, God decides to do a new thing. Twins are to be born. God gives Rebekah advance notice during her difficult pregnancy that the imparting of a blessing to the oldest son will no longer be a mandatory practice. Much as we see the angel prepare Mary for the birth of Jesus, God challenges Rebekah's faithfulness by proposing her involvement in this new thing.

Her pregnancy speaks to the differences in her sons. Even within the womb, they wrestle and war with one another. Then they are born. Esau arrives first, but as Jacob follows only seconds later, he is holding on to the heel of his brother. They are dramatically different in looks as well as temperament. Esau is hairy and loves the outdoors. He is skilled with his hands and thrives on the delight of immediate results from his labors. He is, according to one commentator, a primitive "good ol' boy!"[1] Jacob, on the other hand, is intelligent and intuitive. Unlike his impulsive brother, Jacob writes a five- and ten-year plan with all the action steps to take along the way to achieve his visionary goals. He exhibits the natural abilities and capabilities of leading his clan.

Jacob, however, is also deceitful and cunning. He exploits his brother to gain the family birthright by providing a mess of pottage for the hunger pangs Esau considers urgent. Along with his mother, Jacob also deceives the twins' father. His quest is to be given the family blessing as the youngest son. Here we see in action the thought of the ancient world of the Hebrews that once a word is spoken it cannot be retrieved, as it takes on a life of its own. And so, in hearing Isaac pronounce that Jacob is to be the blessed son, Jacob sets into motion an irretrievable series of events that will mark his life forever.

When Esau hears that his brother has stolen his inheritance, he responds with characteristic immediacy. He determines that he will do what he does best. He announces that he will kill his brother for deceiving their father and betraying their sibling relationship. With the family divided, Rebekah helps Jacob escape.

One of the most honest looks we have of Jacob occurs on his first night away from home. He is in hiding like a fugitive. He is away from his mother for the first time. He has no protection and is, unlike his brother, unskilled in defending himself from the elements of the wild. He is confronted with his guilt, his anger, and his fear. In his mind, he begins the long list of "what if . . ." questions that plague us in the darkness of night.

Then he dreams of a ladder that descends from heaven. He finds that God stands at the top. In a place where Jacob least expects it and at a time when he least deserves it, God appears to him and gives the assurance of divine presence. It is one of those moments wherein we realize that God's grace and promise is as undeserved as our birth and is as available as the breath we breathe. Here, at the end of his rope, Jacob is confronted so that he knows he is not out of every resource. John Claypool says of Jacob's predicament, "Our extremity is often God's opportunity."[2] So in a moment of complete desolation, we find Jacob, and ultimately ourselves, faced with the comforting dynamic that God will be with us on the extreme edge of life as an abundantly grace-filled presence who brings blessing.

Jacob journeys the next day to his uncle Laban's tribe. There he meets the love of his life, but through several events in which the deceiver is deceived, their marriage is delayed. Through his years of labor for Laban, Jacob acquires two wives and numerous concubines. He becomes father to eleven sons and builds his wealth until he finally has enough to risk the return trip home.

Aware that his brother Esau's last words were that he would kill Jacob, Jacob becomes concerned when he hears that Esau is coming to greet him with an army of 400. So Jacob, ever the shrewd one, sends the defenseless women and children ahead to greet and soften up his brother. Jacob delays and spends the night alone beside the river Jabbok.

This situation's familiarity should capture our attention immediately. Because we know what happened before when Jacob experienced a lonely night to face the realities of his relationship with his family, we sense the foreshadowing and foreboding of another night with an unexpected visitor. At first, neither the reader nor Jacob knows the identity of his assailant. The wrestling match is of an inhuman length and brutally painful. No amount of training at the gym could have physically prepared Jacob for this match. While Jacob would have preferred a hearty slap on the back, a mysterious being grants him a wrenching experience that leaves him limping.

This wrestling match with God in the darkness mirrors Jacob's prenatal wrestling match with his brother Esau in the darkness of the womb. Jacob is faced with the truth that struggle with brother and struggle with God are one and the same. These struggles birth him, and us, into a new day. Like Jacob, we may enter it limping, for the battles often leave us scarred and mended, but there is blessing in the forgiveness that is imparted.[3]

It is, after all, forgiveness that Jacob saw in the face of God. We know this because of his encounter with Esau later in the day. The immediacy that so strongly characterized Esau earlier showed itself again. This time, the trait was positive, for Esau was not capable of thinking about anything long enough to allow it to fester within his spirit. So when Esau approached Jacob, there was no malice, no lingering hatred, only a genuine greeting of brotherly love. And when Jacob saw the forgiveness in Esau's face, he recognized it as being the same expression on the face of God. He commented, "to see your face is like seeing the face of God."

This Old Testament story sheds significant light on 1 Peter's command to give a blessing. Following the example of Christ and remembering the symbolism of our baptism, we know we have been cleansed and renewed for a life that gives witness to humility, gentleness, fear, and reverence. This type of response from those who are the brunt of criticism, abuse, or poorly chosen humor is powerful in touching the hardest of hearts. It is what I am beginning to understand as the "Jesus twist." By this I mean the punch the gospel delivers when we realize the despised care the most and the condemned are the most effective when it comes to saving others.

The congregation I am privileged to serve is often in the lime-light of our local association's controversies. True to the experiences of many other Baptist churches who offer refuge to anyone who seeks to worship Jesus Christ, serve with an open Communion pol-icy, ordain women to the diaconate, or call women to serve as a minister on their church staff, my congregation has been called before the membership committee of our local association. While most of these meetings are cordial and border on kindness, every now and then a larger picture of dissatisfaction is presented. I must admit that I continue to be confused over why we are such a threat, why our attempts to be loving create such fear, or why my presence as pastor can be so infuriating.

This is, however, where our experiences find kinship with Jacob. Being a Baptist these days feels like Jacob must have felt with Laban. It is a lot like living in a foreign land, laboring for love, only to be wooed by deceit. We have wrestled into many nights holding on and demanding a blessing from those whose identities are unclear and who ultimately possess no authority.

We have lived with the hope that blessing would come. We have prayed for healing and reconciliation. We have even asked the Lord to show us where we need to seek forgiveness and over what we need correction so that these assaults of spirit might be removed. We have been optimistic that our big Baptist family could find strength in a greater diversity and that we could attempt cooperative ministry. Like Jacob before his reunion with Esau, we are coming to the con-clusion that there will be no blessing.

Like Jacob, we have wrestled and struggled, sometimes fighting with what appears to be superhuman ability. Jacob held on, seeking the mysterious stranger's name and begging for blessing. But look closely! When does the blessing come? Is it in the hard grasping hold of two wrestlers? No! Blessing comes when the mysterious stranger lets go of Jacob. Blessing comes when God touches Jacob's hollow place and marks him for life. Blessing comes when Jacob looks into the face of God and discovers forgiveness.

Seeing forgiveness in God's face helps Jacob recognize the same holiness in Esau's face. These were brothers of the same womb, yet enmity and fear had marked their relationship. When they were reunited and Esau embraced Jacob with forgiveness, Jacob saw God reflected in his brother's face.

I do not know if we will live to see the day when those with whom we have been born Baptist will ever embrace us. I do, however, have expectations of myself and of my congregation. If the maxim for Jacob's life is true—that our extremity is God's opportunity—then how might we be open to the opportunities at hand?

We have a challenge before us in which we can live up to our accuser's expectations or we can, with God being our helper, live under divine expectation. This is the challenge Peter presented to those believers so long ago. It becomes our challenge as well to act out of grace, to be so powerful with our forgiveness and kindness that our words and presence will undeniably be of a holy source. We must not fall prey to anger, give in to fear, start a crusade, or walk away in frustration. We must stay the course; be found faithful; and have a good, positive word to speak. We can do these things because of the grace-filled presence of God that not only wrestles with us at night, but also walks with us during each day so that we might impart the blessing God has given to us.

When my congregation became aware of our status, or lack of, within the association, on their own initiative during the hymn of invitation, they left their seats to walk down the aisle and bless me with words like these: "Be strong!" "Thank you for making a stand for us!" "We love you!" They blessed me by laying their hands on me, hugging me, and praying with me. They blessed me by putting physical presence on a holy presence that is rarely seen. Their faces reflected the Spirit of God who gives blessing through forgiveness and an understanding of grace that I have never experienced anywhere.

Their support reminds me that, ultimately, the blessing for which we all scramble is the one that comes from our relationship with Jesus Christ. At the cross, we find that he touches all of our hollow places in order to fill us with wholeness and healing. Like Jacob, like Jesus, like Peter, we will bear the scars of our struggles, but by those scars we are also freed to step into a new day with hope and promise and blessing.

Prayer

God, be in our head and our understanding.
God, be in our eyes and in our looking.
God, be in our mouth and in our speaking.
God, be in our heart and in our thinking.[4]
God, be in our blessing and in our being blessed.
Amen.

Exercises for Spiritual Reflection

1. A rabbinical story records that when God made the world, God planned to put sparks of light into everything. The holy light was stored in vessels, but it was so strong that the vessels broke into millions of pieces. People were created to find the shards and bring them together to restore the vessels, thereby "repairing the world." Dr. Rachel Naomi Remen, in her book *My Grandfather's Blessings*, writes that we restore the holiness of creation through our loving-kindness and compassion, and every act, no matter how big or small, repairs the world. "We are all here . . . to grow in wisdom and to learn to love better."5 How do you see your personal world (or the larger world) in need of repair?

_____

_____

_____

_____

_____

_____

_____

2. David Bruner and Karen Drucker have written:

> You are the heart.
> You are the hands.
> You are the voice of the SPIRIT on earth,
> And who you are and all you do is a blessing to the world.

How might you fulfill this prayer so that you are a blessing to the world?

_____

_____

_____

_____

_____

_____

_____

3. At the funeral of a church member's mother, it was said that in her last days, the mother lost her memory. When her son came to visit, she could not tell him his name or how she knew him. All she knew was that he was a "safe" person with whom to be. As this son stood in the room while the doctor examined his mother, it became apparent that the mother did not know who she was or where she was. The one identifying thing she did know, however, was whose she was. For when the doctor asked what she could remember, she quoted Psalm 23 from beginning to end. First Peter 3:15b encourages us to be ready to make a defense to anyone who asks about the source of our hope. In the space below, put into words the essence of your faith. While Peter refers to this as our defense, he also encourages us to be prepared so that our answers will reflect the spirit of Christ; therefore gentleness and reverence must be present.

_____
_____
_____
_____
_____
_____
_____

4. Baptists believe baptism to be symbolic of waters that cleanse and renew us. While we are saved through the power of the resurrection, our baptism is often the reference point used to signify the beginning of our walk with Christ in newness of life. In the last verses of chapter 3, Noah is referenced and thus brings to our attention the powerful symbolism of water and its saving power. Consider your baptism. Do you remember it? Record what you remember. If not, how would a revisit to those waters prove meaningful to you now?

_____
_____
_____
_____
_____
_____

NOTES

[1] John Claypool, "JACOB: Writing Straight with Crooked Lines," preached at St. Luke's Episcopal Church, Birmingham AL, 26 September 1990.

[2] Ibid.

[3] Kate Penfield, "A Cup to Hold God's Grace: How God Is Forming Us," *Pulpit Digest* (July/August 1998).

[4] "God Be in My Head," John Rutter's arrangement from *Sarum Primer*, 1545, found on *Be Thou My Vision*.

[5] Jane Breskin Zalben, *Let There Be Light: Poems and Prayers for Repairing the World* (New York: Dutton Children's Books, 2002).

5

Practicing Hospitality

1 Peter 4:7-11; Matthew 10:40-42;
Hebrews 13:1-2

I am a lover of children's stories. One of my favorites is written by Marcia Brown and titled *Stone Soup*. It is a story of three French soldiers making their way home after a war. They are tired and hungry, so when they see a village nearby, they become hopeful that some of the residents will feed them and allow them a place to sleep. As the soldiers approach the town, however, the villagers also spot the soldiers. They are just beginning to recover from the effects of the war. They collectively decide that they do not want these soldiers to take what they have, and so they hide all of their produce, meat, and bread.

The soldiers approach peasant after peasant. "Do you have a room to spare?" "Do you have some food to share?" The answer is always the same: "It has been a poor harvest. We only have enough for our family."

Hearing this many times, the soldiers determine that they will have to come up with their own provisions. They will make stone soup! Since the villagers have so little, they will make enough for everyone to share. So they borrow a huge black kettle. They place three round stones within and fill it with water. As the water begins to steam, they talk about how good their stone soup will taste. While the stones will season it just right, it might possibly taste even better with a little salt. One of the curious bystanders volunteers that they have some salt to spare, so the salt is added. The soldiers begin to remember how they made this soup for the king and that a little cabbage made all the difference. If only they had a cabbage .
. . . Again, a bystander volunteers a cabbage or two and rushes off to retrieve them from a storage bin.

On and on the story goes until, at last, onions and meat, barley and milk, carrots and potatoes have all been added to the soup.

Tables and chairs arrive. Wine is pulled out of cupboards, fresh bread gets taken from ovens, and before they realize it, the town has assembled for a celebration. There is music and dancing and singing on into the night, and the best beds in the village are offered to these three soldiers in the end. The next morning, they are up and gone, and the villagers are left to wonder about the secret ingredient that made the stone soup so delicious.

Hearing this story, we are keenly aware that the key to the stone soup is the fellowship and hospitality the characters enjoy. To me, this story is a parable for teaching hospitality much as hospitality is consistently taught in the Bible.

According to Hebrew Scriptures, hospitality was not an option. It was a matter of justice. This imperative of justice is to care for those who have no right to claim our kindness and hospitality. In other words, we are to behave toward others as God has behaved toward us. We are, then, to be compassionate toward those who have no claim on our compassion. This is especially true when extending hospitality to strangers. Deuteronomy 10:19 says, "You shall also love the stranger, for you were once strangers in the land of Egypt."[1]

The New Testament also places a premium on hospitality. When religious leaders accused Jesus of "welcoming sinners and eating with them" (Luke 15:2), their concern was that Jesus extended hospitality to the wrong people. When the small boy shared his lunch of two fish and five loaves of bread, the miracle was not the feeding of thousands. The miracle was that this child was willing to share his lunch at all. It was a miracle of hospitality.

When Paul criticized the Christians at Corinth for letting the poor go hungry when celebrating the Lord's Supper, he was accusing them of a breach of hospitality. The author of Hebrews even says hospitality is important because some have "entertained angels without knowing it" (Heb 13:2).

The fourth chapter of 1 Peter gives a before-and-after picture of behaviors that may characterize a faith community. Before becoming Christians, the community might be known by their vices associated with idolatry (v. 3). However, after becoming Christians and in spite of taunting or encouragement to join in their "old" behaviors, the Christian community is encouraged to be so filled with grace and wisdom that others will be led to convert. In fact, verses 8 and 9 are directives to practice love and hospitality ungrudgingly so that God will be glorified. While verses 7b through

11 list many things that strengthen the faith community, love and hospitality are the hub. They govern all relationships and stand in direct contrast to the abuses these particular believers have been experiencing as inhabitants in a strange land.

In the tenth chapter of Matthew's Gospel, Jesus teaches his disciples about hospitality. In its beginning verses, Jesus calls his disciples to large and demanding tasks. They are to heal the sick, raise the dead, preach in the streets, and cast out demons. They are sent without money, bags, or even a change of clothes. In other words, they are entirely dependent on the hospitality of those they would encounter.

It reminds me of the Buddhist custom of seekers spending at least one year of their lives as beggars. They go from village to village wearing nothing but a saffron robe and owning nothing but a begging bowl. They must ask and depend on perfect strangers to supply their most basic needs. After that year, they are free to return to their former ways of life, but no one returns the same person. Think of how we would change if we actually had to live dependently on God rather than just talking about it! Think about the understanding that would come from realizing that reliance on God is equal to reliance on the hospitality of others. Think about how we would not be bound by anything—not money, not shoes, not even a walking stick—but yet provided with everything we really needed like healing, forgiveness, restoration, and resurrection. So in reality, Jesus sent his disciples with the only things they really possessed and needed. And it is just as well, for kindness, healing, and forgiveness are the only things the world really needs.[3]

I don't know about you, but these are commands that scare me to death. I have never been successful when attempting to cast out demons or heal the sick. Many times, I would rather stay in the comfort of my pew than take the gospel out into the streets. My choices testify to the fact that I prefer pampering my family to being concerned with those who are starving. And I always respond better to praise than persecution.[4] So I am grateful when Jesus takes a change in venue in these last verses of chapter 10 and says a cup of cold water given to a parched throat will do the trick just as well! This is something I can do, I think.

There is a story about Saint Francis of Assisi, who went to assist the townspeople of Gubbio.[5] It seems that a wolf was terrorizing and devouring the residents when they dared to leave their city's gates. So Francis and his companions went to speak to the wolf. As they approached the forest, the wolf came charging out of the woods bristling and baring his teeth. But Francis called to him to come in the name of Christ. Francis explained to the wolf that he had been killing and frightening the people of Gubbio and that this was against God's law. The wolf then explained that there was no more food in the forest and he was hungry. So to make peace, Francis took the wolf back with him to the town square. He preached a sermon on God's love and mercy. Then the wolf agreed to stop terrorizing the people, and in return the people agreed to feed the wolf. Thus, until the wolf died, they lived as companions. The wolf received his meals and the people lived without fear.

This is the essence of what Jesus means when he says to share a cup of water. The world is frightening when we move beyond our walls of security, and we do not have any idea about what lies in wait to devour us. It is much like Peter's audience living as "aliens" in a foreign land. Yet we are called to reach out to our brothers . . . to reach out to our sisters . . . to reach out to our neighbors who are hungry. We are to welcome and engage those who are lonely. We are to touch the wounded. And we do so in order to extend hospitality and to make peace. There is no other way to do it than face to face, hand in hand, person to person. It involves the risk of rejection, the risk of laughter, the risk of tears, and the risk of love—for others may not like us. They may refuse our offers of kindness. They might wound and persecute us. And scariest of all, they might change us.

While on a mission trip in Africa, we were the recipients of marvelous hospitality. Missionaries on campus prepared a wonderful chicken curry dinner; Mt. Meru university had an appreciation banquet where we were honored guests; and native friends spent an entire day cooking to prepare a meal of local delicacies. When we visited in the churches, we were asked to sit up front so that we would face the congregation. The service would be conducted, and at its conclusion, women came in bearing platters of fruit, baskets full of bottled drinks, and pots of steaming rice and boiling stew. The entire congregation would remain seated while we were served, and they watched while we ate. Only when we handed our empty plates back did they begin to disassemble and stand in line to be fed themselves. Knowing that the water used to prepare these meals was not filtered, this hospitality was a challenge to our intestinal fortitude in more ways than one!

Our first day of HIV testing occurred on a Saturday. We began at Mt. Meru University, testing students and their spouses. We broke for lunch and were then driven to a nearby church. Rains the week before had washed out the road on the last leg of the trip. So we gathered our backpacks and walked the rest of the way through banana and coffee fields. We could hear the congregation singing before we could see the church. We set up for testing in a mud and stick house that was the previous sanctuary. The floor was packed dirt and the hand-hewn benches upon which we sat were about 6 inches wide. After testing the pastor before the congregation, we began testing the membership. We found only one positive case—a pregnant mother.

After three hours of testing, we were fed. Then, as darkness began closing in around us, we packed up our things and said farewell. A full moon was rising beside Mt. Meru as we walked back through the fields to our transportation. The children followed and watched and sang to us as we made our way through the banana and coffee fields.

We were quiet on the trip back to the missionary guesthouse. Mainly we were tired. But we were also reflective. We were overwhelmed by the graciousness with which we had been received. But when we arrived at the guesthouse, we were surprised to receive yet more hospitality. One of our group members, who had stayed behind, greeted us with hugs at the door. Another was full of curiosity about the details of the day. And there was one who, without any pretense at all, went from one friend to another on her hands and knees. She gently removed our shoes, placed our feet in a pan of cool water, and rubbed away our weariness, bringing refreshment, providing comfort, and practicing hospitality.

We did not cast out any demons that I know about that day. We did not heal anyone of his or her infirmities. We only offered and received meager acts of hospitality, and in so doing, we took the risk of finding salvation. This is the great irony of the gospel: when we reach out, open our hearts and souls, receive and offer the grace of God in the smallest of ways, we encounter one another and build the community known as the kingdom of God as we share the hospitality God has already offered us through Jesus Christ.

Prayer

O Lord our God, give us the grace to act hospitably. Just as you have filled our begging bowls with grace, mercy, forgiveness, and love, let us be your agents of hospitality in our places of service with our various gifts. Let us be proactive in reaching out to others to help them find a place of belonging. Let us be gentle in finding paths filled with peace. And let us encourage others with your comfort and goodness. Amen.

Exercises for Spiritual Reflection

1. When you make "stone soup," what are the key ingredients? (In other words, how do you best show hospitality?)

_____

_____

_____

_____

_____

_____

2. Read 1 Peter 4:7b-11. List the activities mentioned that strengthen the faith community.

_____

_____

_____

_____

_____

_____

3. If the list above serves as the spokes of a working wheel, how do love and hospitality work as the hub?

_____

_____

_____

_____

_____

_____

4. Who are the "aliens" in your life? Who stands in need of receiving a cup of cold water?

_____

_____

_____

_____

_____

_____

5. First Peter 4 continues to speak of the varied gifts we each receive. Consider your gifts. Should someone come to you with a begging bowl, with what would you fill it?

_____

_____

_____

_____

_____

_____

6. The following story provides another way to consider the idea of the begging bowl. Read it and then write a list of the things of which you need to empty yourself so that your bowl is ready to receive the hospitality of God.

A wise Zen monk lived in a remote area. An earnest student made his way on pilgrimage to see this teacher.

The serious student, his head filled with questions, became annoyed when the teacher refused to answer his many questions.

"Pour me a cup of tea," the monk eventually said, "and I will tell you when to stop."

The dutiful student started to pour the tea, and he poured and poured. The bowl filled, and he watched with horror as the tea spilled out of the cup and ran all over everything. Exasperated, the student spoke with courage. "Can't you see that the cup is full? It can hold no more!"

"And so it is with you," the wise teacher answered. "Your mind is full of too many things. Only when you are empty will there be room for more knowledge to come in."[6]

_____

_____

_____

_____

_____

Option: A Group Experience

Materials: Nine slips of paper for each participant (each 8 inches long and 3/4 inch wide); pens and/or pencils, tape or glue

On three slips of paper, ask the participants to write things they have given up or might give up that characterize their life outside of Christ. Make a three-link chain by securing the ends of the slips of paper with tape or glue.

On the next three slips of paper, consider the aspects of worship, prayer, mutual support, and celebration that a faith community is asked to develop. In what areas does your community of faith need to focus? Write these on the slips of paper and join them to the paper chain.

On the last three slips of paper, consider your own hospitality. What must you give up in order to be fully used by God to practice hospitality? What might you do to encourage hospitality within your community of faith? In what new ways are you willing to be used by God to show hospitality? Write these on the last slips of paper and join them to the rest of your chain.

Finally, connect the chains of all the participants to form one long chain.

Ask the group to place the chain around them. They will need to move close together so that they are bound by the chain. Say a prayer asking God to give you the power to live freely and without fear of persecution, to rejoice in God's glory and not be dependent on the approval of anyone else.

After prayer, ask the participants to break the chain as they step away from the group. Allow this to symbolize that while Christ's sufferings have set us free, as a community of faith, it is our love for one another, which we show through hospitality, that binds us together. Then ask the group to put their arms around one another, binding them to each other. Request that they voice sentence prayers based on their hopes for ways your group can continue to build and grow as a community of faith.

NOTES

[1] J. Barry Vaughn, "Making Room for God," *The Minister's Annual Manual*, ed. Rebecca H. Grothe, 26 June 2005, 413.

[2] Ibid.

[3] Barbara Brown Taylor, "Heaven at Hand," *Bread of Angels* (Cambridge MA: Cowley Publications, 1997), 154.

[4] William Willimon, "Risky Business," *Pulpit Resource*, 26 June 2005.

[5] Ibid.

[6] See Sue Bender, *Everyday Sacred: A Woman's Journey Home* (San Francisco: HarperCollins Publishers, 1995).

Practicing Hospitality

Greeting with a Kiss

It was one of those rare years when Christmas fell on a Sunday. Being fanatical about Christmas *and* about church, my parents tried to help us, as their children, come to an understanding of why worship services should be held as usual. Hearing this, we were horrified! We would have to give up our treasured Christmas morning traditions in order to be at church!! We begged our Dad to call off services just this once. But he would not be moved.

To accommodate the crazy sort of Sunday morning schedule a pastor's family often experiences, we decided to open all of our gifts on Saturday night and only have our stockings to open on Christmas morning. Even with that compromise, our Dad had already left for the church when we awoke on Sunday, Christmas Day.

Once at church, the choir gathered the faithful few together. When we entered into the choir loft and looked out on the congregation, it was obvious why Dad was compelled to have the service. In attendance were all of those who had no family: the widows and widowers, the "old maids," those who were traveling through, the homeless, the medical students, and the single professionals. When Dad greeted them, he announced that for this one Sunday, we were, as a church family, going to interpret the Bible literally. He went on to say that Paul and Peter both encouraged the congregations to which they wrote to "greet one another with a holy kiss." Because it was Christmas Day, Dad encouraged us to revive this practice. At first tentatively, and then with earnest, we moved from our pews and choir loft and began to welcome one another with a holy kiss. As I received kiss after kiss, I began to realize that I was receiving the best Christmas gift possible—a church family who loved me with God's selfless love.

In his closing comments, Peter tucks away a small detail we often overlook. It is the injunction to greet one another with a holy kiss. (Paul says the same in Romans 16:16; 1 Corinthians 16:20; 2 Corinthians 13:12; and 1 Thessalonians 5:26.) Lest we skim over this verse as something extraneous, we may want to consider that, for centuries, the kiss was an integral and precious part of Christian fellowship and worship. The Jews used the kiss as a greeting of welcome and respect. Just as we read of Judas greeting Jesus in the Garden of Gethsemane with the customary kiss of a disciple greeting a rabbi, so the kiss also became known as a sign of deceit and betrayal.

The early church used the kiss as a measure of the believers' sense of community. Tertullian said, "What prayer is complete from which the holy kiss is divorced?" Augustine said, "They demonstrated their inward peace by the outward kiss." And Justin Martyr talked about the holy kiss as it was connected with Communion. To be able to kiss a fellow believer was a sign that all injuries were forgiven, and thus, they were able to come to the table restored in their fellowship with one another.[1]

Those who had no understanding of the meaning of this practice were of course critical. Their misunderstanding of the holy kiss (and no doubt the misuse of the practice) left the church open for attack. Therefore the kiss of greeting was finally banished. Perhaps we should consider reinstating this ancient tradition!

The other words of the chapter, however, provide us with insight into the author's primary objective. It is to provide consolation to those who felt displaced. While the recipients of this letter were resident aliens who comprised a lower class that existed in hierarchial relationships, they find here a promise that at some point they will be exalted and welcomed as people well known, with a warm embrace and a kiss of fellowship.

With the recognition that there is universality in suffering, they may find strength in assisting one another to resist the "devouring lion." (While a familiar image of the end of time, here the lion is used as a word picture of what it is like to be pursued by temptation and live as victims of harassment.) Peter assures his readers that God's intent is not their destruction but their glory.

He emphasizes this fact by using the words that Christ himself will "restore, establish, and strengthen" us through our suffering.

The word "restore" was most commonly used to refer to a bone fracture that was properly set for healing or for the mending of fishing nets for their original purpose. It is a confident message that God will, through our suffering, provide us what is missing, what is needed for mending, so that we may come out on the other side of suffering filled with strength.[2]

My sister-in-law, Diane, is a kindergarten teacher. She is a gift to parents who bring their five-year-olds to school because she realizes the significance of the new phase into which they are entering. Before she ever meets the children, Diane meets with the parents. She talks about her memories of bringing her two children on the first day of school and the emotions that played inside her soul. She was excited about the new things her children would learn but, admittedly, a little fearful of the new responsibilities and expectations that would be placed on her children. She assures the parents that the children handle this new venture much easier than they will as parents! So she also promises that she will do everything she can not only to make it an easy transition for the children, but for the adults as well.

In that light, Diane shares a story with the anxious parents. It is *The Kissing Hand* by Audrey Penn. In it, a baby raccoon named Chester is fearful of leaving his mother and his home in order to go to school. Repeatedly, he asks his mother, "Please may I stay home with you?" To which his mother always assures him that he will love school.

Finally, she tells him a secret. It is a very old secret that she learned from her mother, who learned it from her mother. It is the secret of the Kissing Hand. At this point, the mother kisses Chester's palm and then says,

> "Whenever you feel lonely and need a little loving from home, just press your hand to your cheek and think, 'Mommy loves you. Mommy loves you.' And that very kiss will jump to your face and fill you with toasty warm thoughts." . . . Chester loved his Kissing Hand. Now he knew his mother's love would go with him wherever he went. Even to school.

When Chester arrives at school, he hesitates before going in. But rather than losing his confidence, he takes his mother's hand and kisses it right in the center of the palm. As Chester scampers into the building, the mother holds her Kissing Hand next to her cheek and is filled with the warmth of the knowledge that Chester loves her too.[3]

We have a heavenly Parent who expressed divine love for each of us through hands that were scarred by nails. When we are afraid, when we are lonely, when we are ill, when we are in despair, we have a Kissing Hand that is like no other. Press your own palm next to your cheek. Feel the warmth course through your body as you remember, "Our God loves us! Our God loves us!"

Prayer

O Lord our God, for your love we are truly thankful. For the privilege of casting all our cares upon you, we are truly thankful. For the restoration that comes from being in your presence, we are truly thankful. For we make this prayer in the name of the one who bears the nail prints in his hands. Amen.

Exercises for Spiritual Reflection

1. 1 Peter 5:7 says, "Cast all your anxieties on him, for he cares about you." It is a verse we learn as preschoolers and one that was repeatedly mentioned to me as a "favorite" by those who heard about my participation in this book. Below, make a list of the ways God has cared for you.

_____

_____

_____

_____

_____

_____

_____

2. How do these experiences encourage you to fulfill 1 Peter 5:2-3: "Tend the flock of God that is your charge, not by constraint but willingly, not for shameful gain but in eagerness, not as domineering over those in your charge but being examples to the flock."

_____

_____

_____

_____

_____

3. In considering the suffering "required of the brotherhood throughout the world" (5:9), make a list of those who might be in need of a "holy kiss."

_____

_____

_____

_____

_____

4. Looking at your list of names, how might you share the hope and comfort of God's care? (For instance, who would benefit from a night out while you keep their children? Who would enjoy an afternoon tea party? Who needs dinner brought to their home or enjoyed with your family? Who is far from home and would delight in a care package, i.e., a veteran, a student, a missionary, etc.? Who would find pleasure in a shopping spree or fresh flowers or a simple telephone call?) Write your action plan so that it is doable for you and the recipient. Challenge: Whatever you decide to do, leave a small bag of Hershey's© chocolate kisses with the following verse attached: "Greet one another with the kiss of love."

_____

_____

_____

_____

_____

_____

NOTES

[1] William Barclay, *The Letters of James and Peter*, Daily Bible Series (Philadelphia: Westminster Press, 1960), 331.

[2] Ibid., 324-25.

[3] Audrey Penn, *The Kissing Hand* (Washington DC: Child and Family Press, 1993).

7

The Ladder of Virtues[1]

2 Peter 1:1-15

Second Peter is one of the most overlooked books in the New Testament. Some commentators even say, "It is the least valuable of New Testament writings."[2] Such criticism makes me curious! Just what will we find when we look a little closer?

In the opening verses, the writer is introduced as a "servant of Jesus Christ." This presentation allows us to know the writer as one who understands that he is totally possessed by God. Like any slave to his/her master, this writer believes himself to be totally at God's disposal, and all rights are surrendered to God. This author was willing to be unquestionably obedient to the commands of his Master and would be in service consistently. There was no time off, no holidays—only time spent serving the Master. So we discover the author as one whose attitude is to offer all of who he is, his time and gifts, in service to God. It is a daunting example!

The writer does this willingly because he has knowledge of God's nature. He is not referencing book knowledge but knowledge of another that comes only through personal relationship. It is a growing knowledge that results from a day-to-day relationship of working with another through committed service. Therefore, our writer does not have a distant or stagnant relationship with his Master. Rather, he enjoys a vibrant knowledge of the one with whom he is in constant communication.

He is writing to those who have "obtained a faith of equal standing" (1:1). This phrase was usually reserved for those who, even though they were strangers and foreigners, were given complete citizenship with all of its privileges. It is recognition that Gentiles were once despised and considered "less than" by the Jews, but in the kingdom of God all are equal through grace.

This equality is further exemplified when Peter is referred to as "Simeon" (1:1). The only other time Peter has this name in Scripture is when he and Paul stand before the Jerusalem Council in Acts 15:6-12. In this account, the Jews question both Peter and Paul for taking the gospel message to the Gentiles. This was a problem for the Jerusalem Council because it took the gospel beyond Jewish boundaries. For Peter to be referred to as "Simeon" here, then, is a clue to us to remember a time when Peter was a mover and shaker, helping the Jews broaden their horizons to include the Gentiles.

In these first verses, then, we know that through this writer's eyes, Jews and Gentiles have equal standing. Through Peter, we watch as the doors of faith are opened to the Gentile centurion Cornelius, to the council in Jerusalem, and now to all the churches who will read this letter.

In verses 3 through 11, the author gives a list of virtues to which believers are to aspire. It is a challenge for us to build one virtue upon another like the rungs of a ladder. We are to strive for the higher rungs as we step on the lower rungs first. Below is a beginning definition for each of the virtues. In the exercises at the end of the chapter are opportunities for you to grow in your personal understanding and create a working definition of each virtue. The following definitions are taken from William Barclay's commentary.

- *Faith:* The unquestioning certainty that the way to happiness and peace is through Jesus Christ.
- *Virtue:* Possessing the courage and integrity to show to whom we belong.
- *Knowledge:* Practical knowledge consists of the facts that allow us an understanding of what to do and how to respond in particular situations. When a spiritual dimension is added to knowledge, it allows us the ability to respond in honorable ways.
- *Self-control:* While our instincts and passions often govern us, the believer with self-control is able to maintain control of him/herself at all times.
- *Steadfastness:* Regardless of what comes our way, steadfastness is the ability not only to face our challenges with bravery and courage, but to maintain a vision that moves us forward. This is true in even the worst of circumstances.
- *Piety:* This is the correct worship of God that leads us to serve others. It does not include "God talk" or the "language of Zion."

- *Brotherly Affection:* Our care for others is so great that the demands that come with personal relationships are rarely a bother or interruption.
- *Christian Love:* This is the culmination of all virtues. It is a love that is as inclusive as God's love.

My first place of service was as a youth minister in a neighborhood church. The responsibilities that come with any staff position were new and challenging for me. In particular, I found that there was an art to budget writing and that the maintenance of the budget required constant attention throughout the year. Our church treasurer, Mr. John, was a daunting man. He had a complete head of white hair and a distinctive voice that rose above any business meeting discussions. He was also fastidiously conscientious in his duties to monitor the budget and church expenditures.

It was his custom to find me at least once a week. He would hold the hair back from my face with his right hand while he tilted my face up toward his with his left hand. He would then look me eye to eye and ask, "So, Shelton, did you take the high road today?" While I was at first puzzled by these inquiries, they soon became our code language for shared ministry that was characterized by excellence and integrity, love for the church, and love for one another. When I could answer confidently, "Yes sir!" Mr. John would put his arms around me in a big bear hug and encourage me to keep up the good work.

Somehow, I imagine Peter extending similar interest and encouragement to each of us as we strive to climb the ladder of virtues. Have we striven for excellence in the virtues of our faith? Have we treated one another as equals and as cherished individuals in the eyes of God? Does our service show complete dedication to God and to one another? Have we taken the high road?

Prayer

O Lord our God, our desire is to practice faith, virtue, knowledge, self-control, steadfastness, piety, brotherly affection, and Christian love. We know this is only possible through your strength. So give us courage. Give us wisdom. And grant us the grace to see others as you see them. Amen.

Exercises for Spiritual Reflection

1. Biblical names carry significance in that they give us, as readers, insight into the nature and character of the individual about whom we are reading. Just as Peter's name took on significance when it was changed to "the rock" by Christ and to "Simeon" when he was before the Jerusalem council, so our names have meaning attached as well. Perhaps you were named for someone in your family, or your name carries a meaning your parents hoped would define you. Consider your name and what weight it carries in your personal perception. What does it teach you about who you are in the eyes of God? Look your name up and find its literal meaning. What insight does this provide?

_____

_____

_____

_____

_____

_____

2. Read the verses listed beside each virtue below. How do these verses help you create a definition that you can own regarding that particular virtue? What other verses help with your understanding of each attribute?

• *Faith:* Hebrews 11:1; 1 Peter 1:6-9

_____

_____

_____

_____

_____

• *Virtue:* Hebrews 13:6; Philippians 4:13

_____

_____

_____

_____

_____

- *Knowledge:* 2 Timothy 1:7; James 3:16-18; James 1:5; Proverbs 3:5-6

_____

_____

_____

_____

_____

- *Self-control:* Psalm 119:11; Ephesians 6:10-11, 16; James 1:2, 3, 12

_____

_____

_____

_____

_____

- *Steadfastness:* Psalm 138:7; Nahum 1:7; 2 Corinthians 4:8-9; Psalm 121:1-2

_____

_____

_____

_____

_____

- *Piety:* Ephesians 5:2, 19, 30; Psalm 55:14; Acts 2:1, 42, 46, 47

_____

_____

_____

_____

_____

- *Brotherly Affection:* 1 John 4:7-8; John 15:12-14, 17

_____

_____

_____

_____

_____

• *Christian Love:* 1 Corinthians 13:4-8a; John 15:9-10; Mark 12:30-33

_____

_____

_____

_____

_____

3. Remembering that each virtue builds upon the other, on which rung of the virtue ladder do you think you stand most of the time? To which virtues do you aspire? What stands in your way? Write out a plan of how you anticipate reaching the top rungs.

_____

_____

_____

_____

_____

_____

Notes

[1] William Barclay, *The Letters of James and Peter*, Daily Bible Series (Philadelphia: Westminster Press, 1958), 355.

[2] Ibid.

Standing in the Thin Places:
A Window to Mystery

2 Peter 1:16-21; Matthew 17:1-8

What we found that day was totally unexpected, but who can predict the presence of God?

I had been asked to be a conference leader for Mercer University's annual pastor's school. It was being held on St. Simon's Island off the coast of Georgia. My husband, Lloyd, was able to take a few days off work, so we drove over together. I was delighted to see that my classes would be in the mornings and evenings so that my afternoons were free. As I left for class the first day, the sun was shining and the ocean was a brilliant blue. But I was surprised to see that the waves were breaking against the rock sea wall right up against our hotel. There was no visible beach upon which we could walk or sun ourselves.

When classes adjourned around noon, I wondered about the beach. Not realizing that the tide would have such a dramatic effect, I was amazed to see sand that extended for about 70 yards. It had been slowly unveiled throughout the morning hours. Lloyd and I put on our jackets and walking shoes and went to walk along the shore. As it was off-season, we had the beach to ourselves.

We had no set agenda. There was no expectation. There was no schedule. It was one of those rare times when our spirits simply rested in being together. So we walked in silence. The mist sprayed in our faces. Occasionally we stopped and picked up a shell. The wind was gentle. The sun was warm.

Gradually, we noticed that the contour of the beach began to change as we approached the side of the island that was closer to the Georgia mainland. While we were standing on what we thought was the shore, we began to see small streams that divided dune after dune. The texture change in the sand, the wildlife that felt free to sit on one dune but not another, and the difference in the water's color all served to educate us that we were walking through an estuary, the place where the mainland's fresh water was coming to meet the sea. It was a place of transition and flux, always different depending on how the tides ran on a particular day.

As the dunes beckoned, we took off our shoes and began to wade across to the outer edges. Finally reaching the last dune and realizing that the water would become dangerously deep with strong currents should we go any farther, we turned around to see that we had journeyed about 150 yards from what we had originally perceived to be the shoreline. Facing the open waters of the Atlantic, Lloyd put his hand in mine and simply said, "It feels like we are standing on the edge of the world."

So we stood there. Still. Silent, with the wind swirling around us as if to capture us in its clutches. To the visible eye, we were all alone. But to the spiritual eye, the undeniable presence and power of our Creator God was very much present. This divine presence kept us rooted to our spot until the tide began to rise, chasing us back toward shore for fear that we would be stranded on the outer banks.

Lloyd and I have never tried to explain that afternoon to one another or to anyone else. Notorious for wanting to talk through and fully understand our shared experiences, this was one time when we simply accepted it as a gift. Over time, I have come to understand such places and such experiences to be what the Celtic Christians would name a "thin place," or a place where God seemed very close and real.

The Celts, inhabitants of the British Isles in the first century, became people of faith due to the influence of Christianity in Europe. They were a mystical, intuitive, experiential group who valued devotion to the Creator of Life, the Christ of Love, and the Spirit of Grace. A major theme of Celtic spirituality was, and is, the immanent presence of God, i.e., that God is everywhere. Being particularly sensitive to God's presence in nature, the Celts were especially attuned to natural places of meeting, places where one area of natural beauty is transformed into another state. For example, where Lloyd and I stood as the land melted into the sea, where fjords and rivers come together, or where water bubbles up from springs deep beneath the earth's surface indicate a meeting of boundaries or a transition from one natural state to another. As places where it is easy to recognize God's imprint and presence, these become areas where we feel strongly connected to God's presence. These are places where the seen and the unseen world seem to be in closer proximity and thus are known to the Celts, and to us, as "thin places."

Gradually, the Celtic Christians began to broaden their understanding of thin places to encompass not only physical locations but to include moments when the holy became visible to the eyes of the human spirit. Thin places, then, took on new meaning for the Christians of this century, for they provided a way to encounter a more ancient and eternal reality within the present time.[1]

Marcus Borg, in his essay "Re-Visioning Christianity: The Christian Life," writes,

> . . . a thin place is any place where the border or the boundary between nonmaterial reality and material reality becomes very thin, virtually transparent, porous, malleable. A thin place is any place where we experience the sacred. A thin place is a place where the veil momentarily lifts, and we behold, [we] experience the Spirit within which we live, and move, and have our being.[2]

Of course, to believe in thin places, we must also believe in the reality that is beyond what we can see, touch, smell, and hear. Thin places mean little, if anything, to those who are convinced that nothing is real that cannot be identified and proven. Thin places elude those with no mind for mystery and who do not possess a longing for the transcendent.[3]

While this idea may seem a bit foreign to us, I would imagine that if we really stopped and thought about it, each of us could point to a place where we can remember God seeming close and real. My hope is that each of us has experienced a thin place—a fragile experience of holiness to which we attach the memory of God's real and close presence. Perhaps your place of spiritual reunion is the beach or the cemetery, your garden or your lake house. Perhaps you are drawn closer to this window of mystery through grand music or silent stillness or the reading of special words. Perhaps you have witnessed the thin places as you provided supportive presence to someone as they died and listened as they called out the names of those long departed but who were also clearly present, waiting on the other side to receive this shared loved one into glory. Whatever the particulars of the situation, these thin places provide believing people a deeper reality of the universe—one that is beyond sight and sound yet is mysteriously tied to Spirit and faith.

Second Peter 1:16-21 refers to what Matthew's Gospel records as the transfiguration of Christ. On the liturgical calendar, this story occurs during a transition time when the boundaries of two seasons meet and enmesh. It is the last Sunday in Epiphany, and Lent begins three days afterward on Ash Wednesday. The Celts would implore us to sit up and pay attention, for it is an opportunity to find ourselves through an encounter with God in a thin place.[4]

In addition, these passages speak of an extraordinary experience. It is an event far beyond the expectations of the ordinary. What we find is a story of amazing transformation in a place of transition. The Celts would inform us that what we read and encounter in our text is a retelling of a thin place, where the veil between this world and the next is so sheer that we watch as Jesus steps right into Holy Presence.

Peter, James, and John accompany Jesus up a mountain so that he can pray. The geographical context alone should get our attention, for it is a place where the natural boundaries of earth and sky collide, a place of transition, a natural thin place. As Jesus prays, his face becomes radiant, a cloud hovers around him, and Elijah and Moses appear with him. Amazingly, the disciples grasp some of the significance of what is occurring. For once, they recognize the privileged view they are receiving of that which is otherworldly and of mystery made evident right before their eyes. So in an attempt to preserve this sacred moment, Peter offers to build three huts.

This is not an unusual response, is it? We often do not know what to do with an experience that does not fit into neatly organized and easily explained categories. We often look for tangible ways to remember or mark the occasion when the intangible becomes reality. Many times, we handle and analyze these experiences until they will make logical sense and lose their mystery in the process.

The reality, however, of what to do with thin places is found right in the Scripture. Matthew records that Jesus asked the disciples not to speak of the event until after the resurrection (as if they could find the words to describe such a vision), and Luke records that the disciples never spoke of it again. Instead, what we find is that they descended from the mountain, and the first thing Jesus did was heal a child who had epilepsy. Rather than placing a historical marker for all who followed to know what happened on the mountain, rather than debriefing so that some sort of mental understanding could occur, rather than establishing a national holiday so that the transfiguration could be celebrated annually, Jesus showed us how to respond to others in such a way that he embodied the thin place. By acting upon the love of God that filled him, Jesus created a challenge to his followers to be transparent, to become the thin place for others as we allow them to see God's love living in and through us.[5]

It was to this that Jesus devoted his life as evidenced by the ways he constantly touched the disenfranchised and by the way he died. It represents a thin place to which we are all invited. For when we think of Jesus hanging on the cross, we encounter a Lord who sacrificed himself in order permanently to bridge the gap between God and us. No more sin. No more law. No more fear. No more distance. For in this thin place, grace creates permeable walls and forgiveness is palpable. It is where love, acceptance, welcome, and rejoicing transform us from one state to another. In this thin place, we do not merely watch as Jesus walks into Holy Presence; we are invited to walk into Holy Presence too. It is where the veil momentarily lifts and we behold this Lord who gave his all for our sakes. In this thin place, we are encouraged and nurtured and sustained with the blood and body of Christ so that we might represent Christ to others through service.

Many of the conversations I attempt with others are met with one-word answers. "How was your day?" "Fine." "How was your meal?" "Good." "How did you sleep last night?" "Okay." We tend to go through each day and get lulled to sleep with the sameness of our routines. Where is our expectation of God's presence? It has caused me to wonder if I need to swap my plan for what another mother does. When she tucks her children into bed each night, their teeth brushed and their hair still damp from the shower, she asks them, "Where did you meet God today?" Over time, they have learned to watch for the thin places so that their answers might be "a teacher helped me, there was a homeless person in the park, and I saw a tree with lots of flowers in it." She then tells them where she met God too, so that before the children drop off to sleep, the stuff of their day becomes the substance of their prayers. They enter a thin place and begin their rest with the presence of God very near.[6]

Prayer

O Lord our God, we pray that you would open our eyes to see you. Open our ears to hear you. Open our hearts to experience your love. And open our hands to serve others in your name. Encounter us, and in so doing, aid us in recognizing you as we enter into Holy Presence and stand in the thin place. Amen.

Exercises for Spiritual Reflection

1. When have you stood in a thin place, in other words, had an encounter with God?

_____
_____
_____
_____
_____
_____
_____

2. Describe what it was/is like to stand in Holy Presence.

_____
_____
_____
_____
_____
_____
_____

3. How can you encourage others to open the windows of mystery?

_____
_____
_____
_____
_____
_____
_____

4. Apparently, the disciples did not share this experience because of Jesus' instructions to "tell no one." Peter finally breaks the silence with his recounting in 2 Peter. What advice would you give others about sharing their thin place experiences? What lessons have you learned from sharing your encounters?

_____

_____

_____

_____

_____

_____

5. How might you allow transparency in your life so that you embody the effects of having been in a thin place?

_____

_____

_____

_____

_____

_____

_____

6. Describe a personal struggle that led you to a thin place. How did the thin place help bring resolution?

_____

_____

_____

_____

_____

_____

7. How would the following Celtic prayer be of help in your personal faith transformation?

May the strength of God pilot us.
May the power of God preserve us.
May the wisdom of God instruct us.
May the hand of God protect us.
May the way of God direct us.
May the shield of God defend us.
May the host of God guard us against the snares of evil and the temptations of the world.
May Christ be with us—Christ be above us—Christ be in us—Christ before us.
Amen.[7]

_____

_____

_____

_____

_____

_____

_____

NOTES

[1] The Rev. Dr. Agnes Norfleet, "A Psalm of Thin Places," North Decatur Presbyterian Church, Atlanta GA, 19 September 2004, http://www.day1.net/printview.php?id=356.

[2] Marcus Borg, "Re-Visioning Christianity: The Christian Life," tcpc.org/resources/articles/revisioning_christianty.htm, p. 5.

[3] Donel McClellan., "Thin Places," First Congregational United Church of Christ, Bellingham WA, 2 March 2003.

[4] Ibid.

[5] Molly Wolfe, "Thin Place," Sabbath Blessings, http://justus.anglican.org/Sabbath-blessings/1999/sb31.html.

[6] Norfleet, "A Psalm of Thin Places."

[7] "Celtic Liturgy: The Final Benediction," http://www.celticsynod.org/liturgy.htm.

Author's Note: This chapter was inspired by Barbara Brown Taylor, "Thin Places," *Home By Another Way.* (Cambridge MA: Cowley Publications, 1999), 57.

9

Waterless Springs
2 Peter 2

In chapter 2 of 1 Peter, we find a theme that is used again in this second chapter of 2 Peter. It is one of "that was then, but this is now." In 1 Peter, the author writes of the comparison of what it was like before the believers had faith. He speaks of being unknown people who had to be called out of the darkness in order to become a royal priesthood and God's own chosen people who live in the light (1 Pet 2:9-10).

In chapter 2 of 2 Peter, we find many Old Testament references that reiterate the theme of this is how it used to be; let us learn from these experiences and choose the different way of righteousness. The writer likens those who know about Jesus and still choose to stay entangled in sin to dogs that turn back to their own vomit or the washed sow who prefers wallowing in the mud (2:22).

Peter begins by pointing out that there have always been false prophets. The new believers should not be surprised, therefore, that there are false teachers among them. Peter's point is that we can remember what the Old Testament prophets told us so that we will not fall prey to those currently trying to lead God's people astray.

The following are general characteristics of false prophets to which Old Testament prophets pointed:

- False prophets are more interested in popularity than in telling the truth. Therefore they often tell people what they want to hear rather than telling the truth. (See Jer 6:14 for an example.)
- False prophets are more interested in personal gain. (See Mic 3:11; Titus 1:11; and 1 Tim 6:5 for examples.)
- False prophets rarely lead pure lives. (See Isa 28:7 and Jer 23:14, 32 for examples.)

- False prophets, ultimately, lead people far away from God instead of closer to God.

With this background, we are not surprised when we read 2 Peter 2:1-3 and realize that the false prophets of which he spoke presented themselves as the authority on truth. Their own private opinions took precedence over God's truth. In addition, they seemed to be motivated by the desire to possess things that were not their own. The blatant disregard for moral rules of conduct resulted in destructive and immoral behavior. They appeared to have no shame, for their acts were public and available for all to witness. They misunderstood grace. Believing it to be inexhaustible and not considering the accountability involved, they felt free to sin as they desired. As a consequence, the reputation of Christianity was being damaged. This type of exploitation only knows a destructive end.

Peter then goes into a long comparison of Old Testament stories. He references the angels, Noah, Sodom and Gomorrah, Lot, and Balaam. These are each highlighted in the study questions, so they will not be dealt with here. However, each is a story of sin and its destructive effects. There is also within each story an element of restoration. These stories include warnings to remain free of the tentacles of sin so that we will not experience waterless springs when in the midst of the dessert.

When my sister was completing her Ph.D. in South Carolina, her daughter, Sarah Helen, often traveled to Evergreen, Alabama, to spend a few weeks with her grandfather. Now an adult, Sarah Helen recently shared with her church family in San Francisco, California, memories from her hot weeks in Evergreen. She said,

> As a child, when listening to the preacher's sermons at his tiny retirement church in the hot, forlorn little town of Evergreen, Alabama, my mind would wander from the Scriptures and complex ramifications presented to whether or not this preacher would please, please end church on time and forgo his afternoon nap to take me swimming. For the Reverend Dr. James Lamar Jackson was my grandfather, and I spent many dusty summer weeks alone with him at our sagging family homestead in humid, tired Evergreen, where his membership to the golf course at the local Country Club gave me conveniently free access to the only swimming facilities in town.
>
> The wait for people to give Granddaddy their thanks and share with him their prayer requests after the service was always

long, and the drive back from the rural church even longer, especially for the indulgent and stifling post-preaching cigar fuming right beside me. He would always wait through the entire drive home, the entire gathering of lunch foods from the garden, the entire preparation of said food, the blessing, and the first few bites before saying thoughtfully, after a long silence, "Well, Baby, I think today might be just the perfect day for a swim."

I don't know why I was ashamed of my mirth, but every Sunday, I would contain it, and reply with practiced nonchalance, "Yes, sir, maybe so. Maybe so."

Dust hung like talcum powder on my moist sweating skin, covered only by my Underoos on those blindingly sunny Southern afternoons, as I plunged myself into cold, chlorinated water, goosebumping my flesh and exciting my senses, while Granddaddy, still in his seersucker suit, praised my diving and swimming from under a poolside table's vinyl umbrella. It was a shivery baptism, the sheer hedonism of it overriding all attempts at respect for Granddaddy's stature.[1]

Think of being like the child Sarah Helen describes—longing for the cool waters on a hot, summer's afternoon, but arriving at the pool to find that there is no water. Think of being in an arid dessert. A fellow traveler assures you that water is just ahead. You arrive at a beautiful oasis and go to the well, only to discover that it has gone dry. Think of running in a marathon. You are struggling, but up ahead you see person after person offering small paper cups of water to encourage and restore you. You take the first cup and the next and the next, only to realize that what each person holds is an empty cup. Such are the "tricks" of false teachers who lead us away from the living waters offered by Jesus Christ.

Following the baptism of two converts at our church, I preached from the baptistery. I took a large pitcher and scooped up the waters from the pool. I leaned down to a choir member on the back row who had a towel. He dried the pitcher, took it in his hands, faced the congregation, and pronounced, "The waters of baptism." As it was passed through the choir and down to the Communion table, each person held the pitcher up and announced the presence of "the waters of baptism."

Once the pitcher arrived at the Communion table, a deacon poured the water into a basin and asked the congregation to consider their own baptism and their personal need to revisit the waters of baptism. The choir stood and sang:

Oh brothers, let's go down
Let's go down, c'mon down
Oh brothers, let's go down—down in the river and pray.
As I went down in the river to pray
Studyin' about the good ol' way
And who shall wear the robe and crown
Good Lord, show me the way.
Oh sisters . . . oh fathers . . . oh mothers . . . oh sinners . . .
Let's go down. Let's go down. C'mon down
Oh sinners, let's go down in the river and pray.

By this time, I had made my way back into the sanctuary in a dry baptismal robe. When the choir finished, I invited whoever had a need to revisit the waters of baptism to come forward. I had no expectation that anyone would come, so you can imagine my surprise when one after another, people moved from their pew to the bowl to dip their fingers, to wash their face or hands, to rub the water on their skin, or to ask me to make the sign of the cross with the water on their foreheads. For some it was merely a time of remembering. For most, it was a defining moment of leaving the old ways behind and choosing to move forward as God's chosen, a royal priesthood, children of the Light.

Prayer

O Lord our God, we thank you for being a spring of living water who invites us to drink deeply and often of holy goodness. Help us also to be sources of refreshment to those who are weary and thirsty. Give us the courage to be examples of virtue and righteousness in the midst of easy and false teachings. For we ask it in the name of one who says we will never thirst if we will but believe. Amen.

Exercies for Spiritual Reflection

1. Read 2 Peter 2:4-16. In this passage, angels are mentioned. William Barclay suggests that "the wicked men of Peter's time were citing the example of the angels as a justification for their own sin."[2] The story they are referencing is found in Genesis 6:1-5 where angels, referred to as "the sons of God," seduce earthly women. The result of these immoral unions was a race of giants whose purpose was to bring wickedness to the earth. These giants gave birth to the *nephillim*, who inhabited the land of Canaan and of whom the Israelites were so afraid (cf. Num 13:33). These giants were accused of being cannibals and were guilty of every sin, in particular insolent arrogance to God.[3]

How is this story an example of sin and its destructive effects? How does it speak to our possibility of being restored to righteousness? What are the commonalities with 2 Peter 2:4-16?

_____

_____

_____

_____

_____

_____

2. In 2 Peter 2:4-16, Balaam is mentioned. Read Numbers 22 and 26 to refresh your memory of the character of Balaam. How is this a story of sin and its destructive effects? How does it speak to our possibility of being restored to righteousness? What are the commonalities with 2 Peter 2:4-16?

_____

_____

_____

_____

_____

3. In 2 Peter 2:4-16, Sodom and Gomorrah are mentioned. Read Genesis 18:22-23 and 19:24-25 to refresh your memory of these cities and their reputations. How is this a story of sin and its destructive effects? How does it speak to our possibility of being restored to righteousness? What are the commonalities with 2 Peter 2:4-16?

_____

_____

_____

_____

_____

4. In 2 Peter 2:4-16, Lot is mentioned. Read Genesis 19 to refresh your memory of Lot's story. How is this a story of sin and its destructive effects? How does it speak to our possibility of being restored to righteousness? What are the commonalities with 2 Peter 2:4-16?

_____

_____

_____

_____

_____

5. In 2 Peter 2:4-16, Noah is mentioned. Read Genesis 6:5-14, 17-22; 7:17–8:1; and 9:8-13 to refresh your memory of Noah's story. How is this a story of sin and its destructive effects? How does it speak to our possibility of being restored to righteousness? What are the commonalities with 2 Peter 2:4-16.

_____

_____

_____

_____

_____

NOTES

[1] Used with permission from Sarah Helen Land's sermon, "Joyful Focus," Metropolitan Community Church of San Francisco, 24 July 2005.

[2] William Barclay, *The Letters of James and Peter*, Daily Bible Series (Philadelphia: Westminster Press, 1958), 380.

[3] Ibid.

10

Session

Waiting on the Lord

2 Peter 3:1-18

Have you considered how much of the liturgical year is spent in waiting? We begin the Christian year with Advent. This is four weeks set aside for personal preparation as we await the birth of Jesus. Then, there are the Twelve Days of Christmas in which we celebrate the birth. This season gives way to Epiphany (the arrival of the wise men). Between Epiphany and Lent is Ordinary Time. Ordinary Time is that long stretch of weeks set aside to wait for Christ to grow into adulthood and to begin the creation of the kingdom of God. We read in Mark that after Jesus began his ministry, he sternly forbade those he healed to reveal the source of their healing. In John, we find the theme that "the time has not yet come" for Jesus to be glorified.[1] So even as Jesus established his ministry and believers were following his leadership, we find that waiting was still involved.

The next season of the Christian year is Lent. As we wait in anticipation for the events surrounding the cross and tomb, Lent prepares our hearts and minds for this ultimate revelation of divine love. With the arrival of Eastertide, we find ourselves waiting once more with the disciples, as the risen Christ commands them to wait in Jerusalem for the Holy Spirit who will encourage and sustain the Christian community as it waits for the second coming of Christ.[2]

This is a return for which we still find ourselves waiting. However, Christian waiting is not like waiting in line for a quick meal or waiting for important papers to arrive in the mail. Our waiting is not passive. It is an active waiting in which we are busy preparing ourselves for the coming of the Lord. With its emphasis on waiting, the liturgical calendar becomes, therefore, a tool or a discipline to use as we continue to grow and be transformed and as we invite others to join us in moving into the future with purposeful possibilities.[3]

This last chapter of 2 Peter deals with the end of time. It is a subject many have spent their lives predicting and speculating over. Others merely dismiss it as the unknown and spend no time thinking of it at all. Peter's approach is somewhere in between. He acknowledges that there are some things we know and of which we need reminding. He also takes a proactive approach in that he gives us things to do while we wait. The end of time does not, however, consume his thoughts as evidenced in his writings.

Throughout this chapter, Peter uses endearing words. Four times, he refers to the recipients of this letter as "beloved." Never does he use demeaning language as if to say they are stupid. Instead, he uses the teaching strategy of repetition. The first seven verses serve as reminders to the community of faith of things they already know. He references the fact that this is his second letter, reminds them of the predictions of the prophets, and emphasizes the commandments of the Lord given through the Apostles. He also includes in this list of resources the writings of Paul. There is a hint of rivalry (and humor) in that Paul's writings are mentioned, but Peter is quick to point out that Paul is often hard to understand! Perhaps the opposition takes Paul's words and purposefully twists them.

While the community of faith's adversaries argue from the vantage that nature is predictable, organized, and orderly, they cannot conceive that the second coming could possibly occur because it would disrupt what is already in place. Peter reminds his readers that we know how unstable the earth is. He cites Noah and the flood as his example. We, especially as recent survivors of Hurricane Katrina, can cite many other natural events, including the tsunami of 2004 in Southeast Asia and the Californian mudslides of 2005, that support the theory that the earth is unstable. Peter's point, however, is that the destruction associated with the day of judgment will be by fire. He argues that our natural world is unpredictable enough for us to believe this will occur.

Verse 8, based on Psalm 90:4, assures that the Lord is willing to give whatever amount of time is necessary so that mercy can be extended to all. Whether it is one day or a thousand years is not the holy concern. Wishing that no one would perish, God will give whatever time is needed so that blessing and salvation might occur.

Finally, in verse 10, Peter describes how he understands the day of the Lord will happen. He says it will happen when we do not expect it, much like when a thief comes during the night. Peter says it will happen with a loud noise. This noise would be so loud that, to make a twenty-first century comparison, it would be much like the roar of a launching rocket ship. Lastly, fire will come upon the earth and dissolve it.

It is important for us to realize that whether we choose literally to believe these verses or not, they serve as a reminder that the world as we know it will not last forever. We are currently in a holding pattern, a waiting time. We wait in anticipation of the day of the Lord.

Should Peter have stopped at this juncture, he would have left his readers hanging. He would have left them with literal devastation rather than the tools to maintain hope. Therefore, fortunately, in the remaining verses of the chapter, Peter continues and gives instructions for how to live out these days of waiting with purpose rather than passive resignation.

As a parent, I learned early that we did not go anywhere without our bag of tricks. Whether we were waiting at the pediatrician's office, or the service was slow at the restaurant, or there was a lot of traffic, we carried our bag of tricks. In it were crayons, coloring books, tapes with music and finger plays, stickers, puzzles, books, paper dolls, crackers, juice boxes, and finger puppets. I was careful to replenish and swap these items out from time to time so that the bag of tricks was never boring. No matter where we found ourselves, the waiting for our children and ultimately for us as parents was made easier because we had things we could do.

Peter instinctively knew how hard it is to wait. So in our waiting for the day of the Lord, he gives goals for us to attempt. These include being zealous in attempting to live without spot or blemish; being at peace; growing in the grace and knowledge of Jesus Christ as Lord; and giving glory to God. An implied mandate from the previous verses would also be that we are given this time to make sure everyone has an opportunity personally to know Jesus Christ. Therefore, our waiting is to be spent in sharing the love of Jesus Christ as well. Being involved in these activities gives us purposeful, positive activities in which to be engaged as we wait. Watching others being faithful in their service not only encourages us but gives us visible reminders of how we should be actively involved as well.

My father was a Baptist pastor. He developed deep, lasting friendships easily. When he served in his last full-time church, he had a dear friend who was in the congregation. The man was a doctor and so was well educated and widely traveled. Both men's children were about the same age, and relationships blossomed among them and between the wives, but my father and the doctor were especially close. Therefore, Dad was concerned when this man was approached about serving as chairman of the deacons, the administrative arm of this particular church, during a particularly challenging year. He talked with the doctor about his fear of losing him as a friend should they work so closely as pastor and a major leader of the church.

Before accepting the position, the doctor took time to consider prayerfully the dynamics of the situation. He went to a jewelry story and purchased two identical tie tacks. On the back of each, he had the word "co-laborers" engraved. He presented one to my dad, and he wore the other one. When they would greet one another or discuss challenges in the church, they would finger their tie tacks as a reminder of their commitment to work together, to bear the load together, and to cooperate together. Because of this visible reminder, they were able to grow in their friendship and in the church.

When my father died, I was not surprised to see this stately, now white-haired man enter the funeral home. He walked to the casket to pay his last respects. As he stood there, I joined him. I reached down and touched his tie tack and simply said, "co-laborers." And the doctor cried.

We need reminders of grace . . . reminders of friendship . . . reminders that keep us going while we are in the waiting periods of life. Peter's second letter gives us such reminders.

Prayer

O Lord our God, in the uncertainty of our physical world, grow the certainty of our spiritual world. Create within us clean hearts, and renew our spirits so that as we wait, our lives will be visible reminders of your mercy and grace. Help us to be patient in our waiting by growing in our relationship with you and with others. Amen.

Exercises for Spiritual Reflection

1. We all need reminders from time to time; thus we make long lists, leave voicemails, send emails, or set an alarm on our computers to remind us of what we need to do. Perhaps the most significant things of which we need reminding rarely happen. For instance, what spiritual truth would serve as a powerful reminder to you? God is love? I can tell others about Jesus? Be ye kind? A soft word turns away anger? God is good? We are co-laborers together with Christ? I am a precious child of God's? In the space below, write simple spiritual truths of which you need reminding from time to time.

_____

_____

_____

_____

_____

_____

_____

2. It might be helpful to transfer these reminders of spiritual truth to slips of paper that you place in strategic areas. For instance, place notes on your mirror, inside a drawer, on your dashboard, in your Bible, as the screensaver on your computer, or on your refrigerator.

Enlist the help of a friend or Bible study companion to remind you of these truths. Ask them to pray that you will incorporate the truths into your daily living. Give them prewritten and pread-dressed reminders to mail to you on dates that they determine and are unknown to you.

_____

_____

_____

_____

_____

_____

_____

Waiting on the Lord

3. When I was pregnant with our first child, the doctor was concerned that the baby would be born with severe handicaps. We had a series of tests performed but had to wait on the results for six weeks. In the end, a healthy baby was born. But those were extremely long weeks of waiting! What are some times when you had to wait? What were the results? How did you persevere? How did you experience God's presence in your waiting?

_____

_____

_____

_____

_____

_____

4. Peter gives distinct advice on ways to wait. How might these be incorporated into your waiting?

_____

_____

_____

_____

_____

_____

5. This book has included many personal stories that have led to faith realities. What stories from your family history have come to mind? How might these stories point you to spiritual truth and fortify your faith during times of exile?

_____

_____

_____

_____

_____

NOTES

[1] Bill Thomason, "Awaiting the Spirit," *The Minister's Manual 2005*, ed. James Cox, (Inver Grove Heights MN: Logos Productions Inc.), 80.

[2] Ibid.

[3] Ibid., 83.

General Bibliography

All personal stories used by permission.

Barclay, William. *The Letters of James and Peter.* Daily Bible Series. Philadelphia: Westminster Press, 1958.

Brown, Raymond E., Karl P. Donfried, John Reumann, eds. *Peter in the New Testament.* Minneapolis: Augsburg Publishing House, 1973.

Mills, Watson E., et al. *Mercer Dictionary of the Bible.* Macon GA: Mercer University Press, 1990.

Perkins, Pheme. *First and Second Peter, James, and Jude.* Interpretation: A Bible Commentary for Teaching and Preaching. Louisville: John Knox Press, 1995.

Summers, Ray. *Hebrews–Revelation.* Broadman Bible Commentary. Nashville: Broadman Press, 1972.

Study the Bible
...a book at a time

T he *Sessions Series* is our expanding set of Bible studies designed to encourage a deeper encounter with Scripture. Each volume includes ten lessons as well as resource pages to facilitate preparation, class discussion, or individual Bible Study.

Now that you have finished your *Sessions with Peter* study, we think that you might be interested in other books from this series.

The following pages contain an excerpt from *Sessions with Corinthians* by series editor Michael D. McCullar.

Coming soon: *Sessions with Timothy and Titus*

SESSIONS *Series*

Call **1-800-747-3016** to order or visit **www.helwys.com/sessions.**

Disunity & Dysfunction

"Where to start?" Paul must have faced this dilemma as he set out to address the questions and issues plaguing the struggling church in Corinth. Disunity is a root disease that over time can literally destroy both the vitality and function of a church. Possibly no other single issue can impact the life and health of a fellowship of believers as this one can. New Testament churches are to be unified in purpose, thought, and love, projecting their "togetherness" to an already fractionalized world. Divided churches are their own worst enemies. How many "yet-to-be reached" people actually want to add to the chaos of their lives by linking with a fractured church?

The Corinthian Symptom

Now I appeal to you, brothers and sisters, by the name of our Lord Jesus Christ, that all of you be in agreement and that there be no divisions among you, but that you be united in the same mind and the same purpose. (1 Cor 1:10)

Modern-day Republicans and Democrats have nothing on the mid-first century Christians in Corinth when it comes to partisan politics. For a small, relatively new group, these Christians were divided into an amazing number of camps. The biblical ideal is to be of "one mind" as Paul writes, but in reality there were multiple minds and opinions in play.

In Corinth there was a natural state of unease between Gentiles and Jewish converts. It was not uncommon in the first-century church for Hebrew believers to view Gentiles as spiritually inferior. There is no doubt that the Gentile Christians lacked the historical and traditional faith experience enjoyed by Hebrew believers.

However, this friction was not the worst display of disunity within this church. Paul's focus was on the splitting up into parties of preference based on the leadership of actual people. "There were four parties or rival factions in the Corinthian Church—a Paul Party, an Apollos party, a Cephas (Peter) party, and a Christ Party" (Dunn, 28).

Anyone who has ever played kickball knows that dividing into teams is a natural part of life. The church, however, is the one facet of life where any such division is counterproductive, even pernicious. Failure is the common result for a divided church, and that was the probable looming destiny for the Corinthians if their disunity remained or progressed.

Parties & Factions

The church had lapsed into taking sides by person—some opting for Paul, others for Apollos, Peter, or Jesus. We will never know the exact reasons for these splits of preference. They did exist, however, and seemed firmly entrenched to the point of creating distinct camps within the church. It is possible that those who opted for Paul had viewed his labor in the founding of the church or had heard of his miraculous salvation experience. The Apollos group was likely drawn by Apollos's oratory skills and intelligence (Acts 18:21). The Peter reference is uniquely puzzling since there is no conclusive evidence that he served in Corinth. He was known to have traveled with his wife and could have visited Corinth at some point. It is also possible that his service with Jesus and success at Pentecost led to a form of fame among early believers.

The Christ group most likely represented those who saw themselves as "super spiritual" due to special blessings or unique insight. It was common for those who had seen Jesus in person to cite superiority in belief, faith, and relationship. This was especially true of Hebrew Christians who accepted Jesus' Messiahship during his earthly ministry. It's easy to see how the self-centered views of this group could have led to discord and division within the church.

Teaching the Corinthians How to Be Wise

Paul's approach to these divisions within the Corinthian church was to begin with the issue of wisdom. The root problem in the church was not their preference of leader or personality; rather it was their lack of supernatural wisdom. The Corinthians had been greatly influenced by classic, rational Greek thought. They were naturally inquisitive, logical thinkers who sought proof on all issues of consequence. This was also true of many Hebrews who had become Greek-like in thought and action due to time spent in Greece and elsewhere in the Roman Empire.

Paul goes on the defensive by simultaneously utilizing and then destroying the use of logic and reason applied to faith in Christ. "Has Christ been divided?" was an illogical picture that forced the Corinthians to see their error in intellectual ways. For a rational, logical thinker, the very thought of a divided person would be ludicrous, which was, of course, Paul's intent from the beginning. Even the Corinthian Christians were familiar with the unique link between the One Christ and the church. Beginning with Christ and extending through Pentecost, the theme of oneness and unity was prevalent. Just as one Christ could not be divided, neither should the church bearing his name be divided. In essence, they are one and the same in all ways spiritual.

> The grounds of our allegiance to Christ, are first, that
> he is the Christ, the Son of the Living God; second, that
> He has redeemed us; third, that we are consecrated to
> Him in baptism. All these grounds are unique to Christ.
> To no other being in the universe do believers stand in
> the relationship that they all sustain to their common
> Lord. As, therefore, there is but one Christ, one
> Redeemer, one Baptism, Christ cannot be divided without
> violating the bond that binds them to Christ and to
> one another (Hodge, 33).

Paul goes on to ask, "Was Paul crucified for you?" No doubt by this second question the Corinthians were saying, "No more, we give up, we get the point!" This question would, however, quickly strike at the center of misplaced priorities. Jesus the Messiah was crucified. Paul the supreme church planter and evangelist was merely a messenger. By invoking the crucifixion of Jesus, Paul reinforced the true uniqueness of Jesus Christ.

The Cure

No epidemic has ever been eradicated without first knowing the source of infection. Find the source and you have an opportunity to create a cure or, at the very least, to stop the spread of infection. The same line of thought could be applied to the Corinthian disease.

The symptoms were manifested by disunity, but the source was clearly inferior spirituality. They were far too human in the ways they approached wisdom and faith. They attempted to apply natural wisdom to supernatural issues. God however, had turned natural wisdom upside down through Jesus and the cross.

In vv. 23-24 Paul cites "Christ crucified, a stumbling block to Jews and foolishness to Gentiles." The Jews had hoped for a Messiah on the order of David. They sought a Messiah of power and might to lead them against Rome in ways both political and military. The Gentiles saw Jesus' death on the cross as extreme weakness and the resurrection as an impossibility. Simply put, only rank criminals die on crosses, and they do not come back to life. So while Paul described Jews and Gentiles who still dismissed Jesus as Messiah, he correctly described their overall tendencies of relying on traditional logic and rational thought.

Step 1: The first step in overcoming disunity is to move away from finite natural wisdom and utilize the gift of supernatural wisdom supplied by the Holy Spirit. James described the two types of wisdom in 3:13-16: "Who is wise and understanding among you? Let him show it by his good life, by deeds done in humility that comes from wisdom. But if you harbor bitter envy and selfish ambition in your hearts, do not boast about it or deny the truth. Such 'wisdom' does not come from heaven but is earthy, unspiritual, of the devil. For where you have envy and selfish ambition, there you find disorder and every evil practice."

James goes on to say that supernatural wisdom is pure and is of God. So we have both Paul and James drawing a line between natural human wisdom and wisdom provided by God through the Holy Spirit. The differences are clear. Faith fueled by natural wisdom leads to dysfunction; supernatural wisdom leads to righteousness. This distinction is clear and is consistently taught throughout the New Testament.

Barrett sees Paul's wisdom as "more than a wise plan; wisdom is not merely the plan but the 'stuff of salvation'" (56). The wisdom provided by God through the Holy Spirit is central to all of our faith thoughts and practices. It becomes the lens through which all else is viewed. It is difficult to default back to natural wisdom when viewing life though the lens of salvation and God's purposes.

Step 2 : The subsequent next step is to practice unity. It is obvious that humankind isn't naturally prone to unity. In fact, the exact opposite would be closer to reality. It is possible, however, for Christians to unify and be like-minded. A word study reveals that Paul seeks unity on the big issues of faith. Barrett writes, "that you may all be agreed in what you say means literally, '*that you may all say the same thing*'" (41).

The divisive issues were squarely major faith issues. Paul stresses the need to "think" alike on the major issues of faith. Another approach would be that there are certain absolutes integral to Christianity. Christians, especially those within a church, must be like-minded in regard to these absolute beliefs if they are to move in God's appointed direction. it is obvious that Christians will not agree on all aspects of faith. Paul knew this and only expected the Corinthians to agree on the absolutes.

Life Lessons

As you will note on your journey through 1 and 2 Corinthians, there is a great deal to learn from the dysfunction and error of the church of Corinth. Chapter 1 provides insight into two potential problems that continue to plague churches. First, we must focus on Jesus and not on the personality delivering the message. Far too many churches have seen the destructive result of people worshiping the messenger rather than the central focus of the message. Christ crucified, risen, and ascended is the foundation for our existence as Christians. If believers move away from that single focus, dysfunction will certainly follow. If on his best day Paul was merely a messenger, then all preachers and teachers should only aspire to the same goal.

Second, believers must tap into supernatural wisdom if God's will and purposes are to be known. There is little room within the life of a Christian for conventional, natural wisdom. That approach to decision making is flawed, temporal, and finite. It is only through the gift of spirit-wisdom that one can know what God purposes for life. Spirit-wisdom is the path to righteousness; natural wisdom is the slippery slope to all sorts of dysfunction, including disunity on a grand scale.

1. Identify ways disunity can damage, even destroy the effectiveness of a church.

_____
_____
_____
_____
_____
_____

2. What are the dangers of following individual church leaders to the point of factions forming?

_____
_____
_____
_____
_____
_____

3. Identify ways in which "inferior spirituality" plays into church disunity.

_____
_____
_____
_____
_____
_____

4. Identify ways people utilize natural wisdom rather than supernatural wisdom through the Holy Spirit.

_____
_____
_____
_____
_____

5. Briefly describe Jesus being a stumbling block to the Jews and foolishness to the Greeks (Gentiles).

_____

_____

_____

_____

_____

6. Identify the "absolutes" on which Paul seems to say all believers must agree.

_____

_____

_____

_____

_____

_____

7. If believers utilize spiritual wisdom as the lens through which life is viewed, how might life change for them as individuals? As a church?

_____

_____

_____

_____

_____

_____

8. Identify ways church disunity has led people who aren't Christians away from the faith.

_____

_____

_____

_____

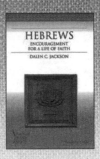
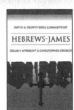